Minimalism

The Life Altering Magic of Organizing, Simplifying & Decluttering Your Life

By Ace McCloud
Copyright © 2016

Disclaimer

The information provided in this book is designed to provide helpful information on the subjects discussed. This book is not meant to be used, nor should it be used, to diagnose or treat any medical condition. For diagnosis or treatment of any medical problem, consult your own physician. The publisher and author are not responsible for any specific health or allergy needs that may require medical supervision and are not liable for any damages or negative consequences from any treatment, action, application or preparation, to any person reading or following the information in this book. Any references included are provided for informational purposes only. Readers should be aware that any websites or links listed in this book may change.

Table of Contents

Introduction 6
Chapter 1: Incredible Decluttering Methods..................... 10
Chapter 2: The Best Organizing Methods 15
Chapter 3: Easy Feng Shui Methods 21
Chapter 4: Mental Release and Meditation Techniques 25
Chapter 5: Secrets to Healthy and Happy Relationships ... 43
Chapter 6: Minimalism Techniques with Technology 50
Chapter 7: Five Items the Minimalist Should Always Have on Hand 55
Conclusion 70
My Other Books and Audio Books 71

Be sure to check out my website for all my Books and Audio books.

www.AcesEbooks.com

Introduction

I want to thank you and congratulate you for buying the book, "Minimalism – The Life Altering Magic of Organizing, Simplifying and Decluttering Your Life."

This book contains proven steps and strategies on how to organize your belongings, simplify your life, improve your relationships, and eliminate negativity and other unneeded things from your life. You would be amazed at the negative impact clutter and unneeded and unhealthy things can have on your life. These things can steal your motivation, leave you feeling depressed and ruin your productivity in a variety of ways. This book will help you simplify your life so that you have less to worry about and are free to live an unfettered life of serenity, peace, and joy.

Minimalism is not just a technique to simplify your life. It is not just a method to keep your house clean and tidy either. The dictionary might say minimalism is a way of getting rid of the excess in life. However, it is so much more than that; it is a way of living fully.

Of course, part of being a minimalist is to rid yourself and your home of things you really don't need and never use. Did you know that about 55 to 60 percent of your possessions are not truly necessary? Minimalism methods can rid you of all that excess baggage. In the process, minimalism creates space for peace, happiness, good health, and an improved mental state. Decluttering, removing what you don't need – from possessions to relationships – is a necessity. It frees you from unnecessary distractions and encourages you to keep only what you love and what you need in order to not only survive, but also to thrive.

If you knew you had to move your household in a week, would you panic? Most people would. They would envision collecting tons of boxes and frantically packing up all their stuff in just a few days while begging others to help them with their massive collection of things that they have accumulated over the years.

On the other hand, a minimalist would have no problem moving in a week. If you are a minimalist, you could pack what you need fairly quickly and easily. The loose ends most of us have to manage would not even exist for them.

Everyone finds it difficult to get rid of their stuff, myself included. It is hard to put perfectly good things in the trash or to give them away and, heaven knows – even though you haven't used something for over a year, you just might need it again 10 years from now. Yet, take another look at that last sentence. Doesn't it sound ridiculous? If you haven't used something in four years, two years, even one year, are you really going to need it again? Probably not.

Most of us live our lives at a pace that would rival time trials at the race track. Many people work long hours, are in debt, are tired, stressed, and feel that they lack everything needed just to survive. By contrast, a simpler life allows us to be content and consistent. If you don't have as much stuff to worry about or to fear losing, you will have more mental energy to do the things you like to do. When you keep only the things that bring you joy, you don't need to work so hard to maintain them.

Some of the benefits of living as a minimalist are:

- That claustrophobic feeling leaves you, because everything is clean, neat, tidy, and everything has its place. Your counters and tables are clear of clutter and you feel like you can breathe easier.

- You have more time to do things you enjoy, including hobbies and being fully present with your family.

- You save money because you avoid buying things you don't need, no matter how pretty and shiny they might be!

- You have peace of mind, because you have less to worry about taking care of and the relationships you do have are worth it.

- You have less fear. Buddhist monks have nearly nothing. Everything they use is owned by the community. Therefore, they have little fear. If it all went away, they would lose little of substance. If you don't have much to lose, there is little fear of losing it.

Here is a good example of the effects of minimalism. John Doe is a single man in his 30s. He is now the CEO of the architectural firm where he started out as one of the architectural draftsmen. He has a five-bedroom house with a home theater and a game room, a four-car garage filled with cars, a swimming pool, and a tennis court. John Doe might be in his 30s, but he is so overwhelmed with his life that he feels like he is 60. He works long hours and makes more money than he can use.

John is old before his time. He worries about losing everything he owns, yet it is impossible for him to sleep in five bedrooms simultaneously or drive four cars at one time. He hates being the CEO of the company and wishes he could just go back to being a regular architect who designs buildings. John is rather unhappy with his life, bet he sees no way off the treadmill.

After surviving a heart attack however, he decides things have to change. He sells his house. He sells all but his favorite car. He quits his job. John takes the money he has earned and starts his own company that designs and builds tiny houses. He has even designed his own tiny house. He now lives in a space that contains a living and kitchen area, a bathroom, and a bedroom loft. He has gotten rid of everything that is not useful or beautiful to him.

Most of the people John thought were his friends have abandoned him, now that he has very little, so only a few relationships remain. These are the friendships that are valuable and lasting.

John lives a simple and happy lifestyle. He goes to work when he wants and is able to pay his bills and buy the food he needs. He coaches a little league baseball team – something he never would have had time for before – and he is making solid friendships and staying healthy.

He no longer fears that he will lose everything, because he has very little and much of what he does have can be easily replaced. His health and his life have improved greatly.

Would you like to live like John? Maybe you want a simpler lifestyle but don't see the need to go as far as John took it. That is okay. The great thing about minimalism is that you can choose how far you want go; you set your own parameters. No one can make the rules for you.

If you get part of your home decluttered and decide to only end one relationship, your life will still become better. You don't have to live in a tiny house or fit all your belongings into a few boxes. The objective is to go beyond barely surviving to full-fledged living. Whatever you do in the form of minimalizing must support this objective.

I suggest you start by setting goals and establishing some timelines, outlining them in the form of objective statements. Here are some examples of objective statements that define one person's decluttering efforts:

- In the next two weeks I will clean out my closet and get rid of all the clothes I haven't worn in a year.

- I will clean out my kitchen cupboards and declutter my countertops in the next four weeks.

- Within the next six weeks, I will get rid of any items in the living room that have no use or do not bring joy to my heart.

- I will spend more time with people who are important to me.

These are just a few examples. You can be more detailed or more general, depending on your level of involvement in the process. You can work at minimalizing your lifestyle a little at a time, or you can dive in and do the work all at once. You make the rules when it comes to pursuing a minimalistic lifestyle. The results are totally up to you.

The following chapters will give you guidelines on how to declutter, organize, and enjoy the things you do keep. You can adapt these instructions in any way that suits your needs and fosters the lifestyle that you want to have.

Because the people in our lives can influence whether we live richly or just exist, I have included a chapter to help you evaluate your friendships and choose which relationships to focus on and which to hold more loosely.

My hope is that after you finish this book you will be able to step back and re-design your life in a way that brings you the most joy, that will allow you to live the most fully, and that equips you to love the most generously.

Chapter 1: Incredible Decluttering Methods

Decluttering is essential to starting a minimalist lifestyle. It might seem a shame to get rid of perfectly good items, but there are several ways to justify decluttering so that you don't feel guilty. You need have no qualms about throwing away things that are worn, stained or no longer useful to anyone. Some of your quality stuff can be passed on to people you know. If a friend has often remarked that he loves a particular figurine, something that's not all that important to you, give it to him so he can enjoy it.

You can also donate items. Goodwill, Salvation Army, and other nonprofits receive donations and accept almost anything. A Habitat for Humanity ReStore will be glad for your discarded household fixtures.

You can always hold a garage sale and make a little bit of money, while getting rid of things you do not need; you can get to know the neighbors in the process. You can always give away or throw away anything left over. You will be surprised what people will take when it is free. Some nonprofits will even pick up your unsold items for their thrift stores.

There are multiple methods available to help you declutter. I suggest you try out several and pick what works best for you. Decluttering does take time. Don't expect to get it all done in one day, but do set goals to guide you through the process. I suggest you use a calendar to mark down each stage of your decluttering and assign them specific target completion dates.

It's easiest to tackle the process one room at a time. Be aware that cleaning out a closet will usually take most of a day or even two days; it's a big job! Decluttering the kitchen is also a one- to two-day job.

Some experts say you should do a little decluttering at a time, giving one item away per day or filling one trash bag in a week. Others say it is all or none. They think you should go through every closet and drawer with clothing in it all at one time so you don't forget what you have.

Remember, you make the rules. If you want to take it slow, take it slow. Just keep in mind that one item a day means it may take your lifetime to complete the decluttering process! However, if you are enthusiastic about becoming a minimalist, get it all done in a week or two and start enjoying your clutter-free lifestyle.

The following are some popular methods of deciding what to discard, with techniques for staying organized during the process:

The 12-12-12 Method

Twelve is a nice round number. It doesn't take long to gather up 36 items and decide what to do with them. To work the 12-12-12 method, you collect things in your house, finding 12 things to put away, 12 things to give away and 12 things to throw away. You can do this once, twice, or three times a week. It's up to you.

The Four Boxes or Baskets Method

Acquire four large boxes that are nearly the same size or go out and purchase four of the same kind of laundry basket. One will be for trash you will throw out, one is for things to give away, one is for things you want to store and the fourth is for things you want to keep. Take a room and start filling up the boxes or baskets. Once you fill them, get rid of the stuff in the trash box, box up the stuff you want to give away, then pack and stash what needs to be stored. Take everything out of the fourth box and ask yourself, "Do I really need this? Does it bring me joy?" If the answer is yes, then put it in its proper place; otherwise, put it in one of the other boxes.

The Mapping and Rating Method

In this method, you make a map of all the rooms in your house. Mark where the doors and windows are located and draw in the closets. Draw where the furniture sets. Rate each room as to how cluttered it is, marking one for uncluttered, two for somewhat cluttered, three for very cluttered, and four for the ultimate cluttered space. Start with the most cluttered room first and take that map with you. Mark with an "X" the most cluttered area and start cleaning out there. You can use your 12-12-12 technique or the four-box method in conjunction with this plan.

The Clockwise Method

This is my favorite method and it can be used along with the previous techniques. In this method you pick a starting spot in a room. If it is in the kitchen, you might start at the stove. Have your four boxes ready and pick up anything you don't use that might be near the stove. For example, let's say you don't use your standalone timer anymore because you use the stove's timer or the timer on your phone. Put the timer in the donate box because it still works just fine.

To the right of your stove is a countertop upon which sets a container full of all kinds of kitchen utensils. You might have six or eight spatulas and three to four slotted spoons. Do you really need that many? Keep two of each and put the others in the donate box, except for the one that is half-melted and very ugly. That one goes in the trash box. Clean off your countertops, putting everything in the corresponding box (trash, keep, relocate, give away).

Then turn the corner to face the kitchen sink and keep going in a clockwise manner until you are back at the stove again. You could tackle the cupboards while cleaning the counters, or you can handle them on a separate rotation, cleaning inside all the cabinets and cupboards. This method ensures that you won't miss something by getting distracted in a random treatment of the room.

The Backward Hanger Method

This method works great with clothing but it can be adapted for books, CDs and DVDs as well.

Take everything out of your closet and decide what you want to keep and what you can immediately eliminate. Next, put everything you want to keep back on hangers, but hang them over the bar with the hook facing the front, what most people would call backwards. After wearing something, wash it and put it back on the hanger, but this time hang it as you normally would – forwards. After three months, get rid of what is still on backwards hangers. Of course, if the unworn clothes are items that are off-season, wait another three months before you get rid of them. After all, if you haven't worn it in six months, you're not likely to wear it at all.

To adapt this to books, CDs, and DVDs, place the items upside down. After three months, review your items and get rid of anything still upside down. Of course, some reference materials may not get used that often and others may be irreplaceable; the choice is ultimately up to you.

Store Seasonal Items

I suppose you will want to keep some items that are used seasonally. You wouldn't use your Christmas decorations in the summer and you probably wouldn't use a beach ball in the winter. In this case, store seasonal items in large plastic tubs that are labeled for easy identification. Store them in the garage or basement to keep them accessible but out of the way. If you're an apartment dweller, I'm sure you can find a handy storage spot, under your bed, in a closet or covered with a cloth as an extra end table.

Here are some ways to tidy up and declutter specific areas in your house:

Countertops

Get rid of small appliances you never use. You may have used that baby bullet to make baby food for your infant, but he now has a full set of teeth and is going to school! You don't need it anymore. Appliances most people use regularly are can openers, toasters, coffee makers and sometimes a blender. Toaster ovens are a necessity for some people. As a rule of thumb, if you haven't used it in a year, you might as well get rid of it.

Linen Closet and Medicine Cabinet

Clear out everything in the linen closet. You won't believe the stuff that works its way back into the corners. Get rid of any worn towels, sheets or blankets and put back in only the ones that are in good condition.

Take everything out of the medicine cabinet and look at the expiration dates. Get rid of anything old. Many pharmacies will receive outdated medications and dispose of them safely. It is not recommended that you throw old medications in the trash nor dump them down the toilet. Someone could pull them out of the trash and try to use them and, if flushed, they could contaminate the water supply. This latter is highly unlikely, but it's not worth taking the chance.

After removing outdated medicines, put anything that is still usable back in the medicine cabinet.

Drawers

Everyone has a sock drawer, an underwear drawer and a junk drawer. You might also have an office supply drawer, a jewelry drawer, a sweater drawer or others. Remove the contents from a drawer at a time and sort through them using the box method. Keep the things you need to keep, placing them neatly back in the drawer or storing them in a better place. Throw away or donate items that you will not use again.

Recipes and Papers to Keep

You want to keep your tax information for at least seven years and you will always need to keep birth certificates, marriage certificates and other important papers. Store these in a file cabinet or a plastic bin, clearly labeled.

With any papers where you don't need the originals, I recommend you scan them into digital storage. Scan your recipes and other papers, storing them in your computer or on the cloud. Scanned items take up no space, they won't yellow or fade, and you can access them much more easily than wading through the physical papers. To minimize the risk of losing these items, keep backups on a jump drive, an external hard drive, or in cloud storage. Scanning your papers will significantly simplify your life.

Preparation and Maintenance

Before you start your decluttering project, visualize how each room will look without the clutter. Believe me, if you do this you will find yourself smiling from ear to ear. Remind yourself of this image while you're in the process and revisit your decluttering calendar frequently so you won't miss a deadline. Weekly review your calendar to measure how far you've come. Keep your focus on turning your visualizations into reality.

Once you get moving on decluttering it can be rather hard to stop. That's a good thing, because once you've finished decluttering, you will need this mindset to keep things decluttered. Maintaining a clutter-free house, however, will be easier after you've gone through this process.

In the future, when you bring something new into the house, use it to replace something that is already there. If you buy two new shirts, for example, go through your closet, find the two oldest shirts you have, and get rid of them.

Before you purchase anything to bring into the house, ask yourself if you really need it. If you do, bring it in as a replacement for something else.

In addition to removing clutter, your life will be enhanced by maximizing the organization of the things you have chosen to keep. The techniques in the next chapter will help you optimize your use of the things you have.

Chapter 2: The Best Organizing Methods

Now that you have decluttered and downsized your lifestyle, it is time to organize your stuff. Hopefully, you will have accomplished a bit of organizing as you put things in their proper place. This chapter will help you optimize the organization of specific things like the paper that comes into the house on a regular basis and the clothing left in your closet. We will even discuss the organization of your car.

Sorting Methods

When you organize, you still need to sort things out. In order to do this, you will need your boxes again to keep like things separate. In your room, you might use a box for pants, one for tops, one for shoes. In the kitchen, you might use a box for baking needs and others to separate oils, cans, boxes, etc. You also need to keep a garbage bag handy for anything you realize you don't need, even after decluttering. To keep things organized, it is important that you place a trash receptacle in each room, not just the bathroom and the kitchen. Place one in the family room, the bedrooms, and any other room in which you hang out.

Papers

The majority of the clutter that enters your house comes in the form of paper. The mail comes every day, so what do you do with it? Often it lands on a countertop or table until you have time to go through it. The kids bring papers home from school and guess where they land; on the counter too, atop or near the mail. If you bring paperwork home from work, it inevitably ends up on the same counter, if it hasn't successfully reached the desk in your home office.

Paper can add up quickly, so we need to tackle this first, before it can quickly grow into another decluttering project. We need a process in place for handling the daily influx of paper.

First off, I suggest you designate a contained area for incoming papers. At the very least, use a plain cardboard box, although even this can be decorated and prettified. Another idea is to place stackable baskets in an out-of-the-way area for processing incoming papers. One could be for incoming bills, another for school paperwork, and a third for things to file, like receipts. Open your mail near these baskets so you can sort them immediately into bills to pay. Immediately throw away the envelopes and inserts in a nearby trash bin. Pitch junk mail in the trash as you open the mail.

Make it a point to file every day or at least a couple times a week, so papers won't start to pile up. Use a filing cabinet or a pocket folder to hold bills to be paid, bills that are paid, receipts, correspondence, and warranties or other records.

Kitchen

The kitchen seems to be a gathering place for junk, probably because of its expanse of countertops. Once you get everything off your countertops, keep it off. Stash tools near where they will be used. Utensils such as spatulas, slotted spoons, pancake turners and the like should be stored in a drawer near the stove. Pots and pans should also be stashed near the stove. Colanders should be near the sink where you will use them. Place your salt and pepper near the stove to make them easily accessible. Keep herbs and spices near where they will be used but away from the heat of the stove to preserve their flavors.

The pantry and cupboards should also be kept in an orderly manner. Put all the boxes together, all the cans together, and contain loose packages of rice, dried beans or other mixes in a plastic container the size of a shoe box, so they do not scatter everywhere. Place items with the closest expiration dates in front, so they will be used first.

Keep an inventory on the pantry door of items inside and cross them off as you use them. This will allow you to see at a glance what you need to stock up on when you're heading out to the store. I keep a paper on my refrigerator door where I jot down items that need to be replaced. The next time I leave for the grocery store, I simply grab the list off the fridge, jot down additional items from the pantry, and I'm good to go. You can also download apps that allow you to keep a grocery list on your phone.

Living Room/Family Room

The coffee table is usually the living room's most cluttered spot. Opt for a functional coffee table that has drawers where you can stash the remote and other items you use there.

Some coffee tables are hollow inside with a lid that allows you to hide newspapers and magazines for later reading. This can also be a great place to store blankets for when you need them in cold weather. Some coffee tables are high enough to slide a basket underneath that stores magazines and newspapers out of sight.

The space behind your sofa is another great location for storing things. You don't have to put your sofa right up against the wall. Instead, use low bookcases or a tall thin bookcase turned on its side so it will be hidden by the sofa. You can easily stash pillows, blankets, DVDs and CDs there for quick access.

Toys

Toys are a constant source of clutter, but there are ways to contain them. Designate a play area in your home that is out of the way of the living area. Put down a brightly colored rug to designate that place for toys. Store toys in plastic bins, a toy box or in baskets.

Your kids do not need every toy they own in the space at the same time. Rotate the toys, leaving just enough to keep them busy in the area, while the rest are hidden in a closet or in a shallow tub under their beds. Every other week rotate some stored toys into the play area and stash some that have been out for a while.

You can also put toys on open bookshelves that mark the perimeter of the play area; just make sure these shelves are anchored to the ceiling to prevent them from falling if climbed upon.

Books laying flat on a coffee table take up too much room and tend to clutter the area. Store all books on a bookshelf to keep them looking tidy, never laying on a flat surface. Store DVDs and CDs, if you have not transferred them to digital storage, in towers made for that purpose or in a bookcase. A hollow ottoman with a lid is another good place to stash them, or you may opt for baskets under the coffee table.

Many people like to collect things. Collections range from figurines of some kind to vinyl records or some such. The philosophy behind minimalism runs counter to collecting, but if you just can't bear to part with your unicorn figurine collection, keep it to a minimum size. Display your collection in a shadowbox on the wall so as to avoid cluttering a flat space. Another option is to place them on bookshelves in front of the books. A glass china cupboard will also enclose your collection so it doesn't get dusty or damaged.

Bathroom

Bath towels take up a lot of room in the bathroom. To maximize bathroom space, roll them lengthways and store them standing on end in a basket. This will leave more room for other bathroom essentials. Extra sheets and blankets are easily stored in plastic bins in the linen closet, allowing you to keep them folded neatly and dust-free.

If you have too many people for your towel racks, stand a ladder against a wall and hang each person's towel on a rung. You can also screw hooks into a wall, one hook per person.

The space above the toilet is often wasted. Find the type of shelves that fit over the toilet and store baskets of towels on them. You can also put swabs, cotton balls and little soaps in glass jars on these shelves.

Makeup and hair care products can easily clutter a bathroom counter. Keep hair care items in a bin under the sink and make sure to get rid of anything you don't use regularly. Store makeup in a bin in a linen closet or in drawers in the bathroom and only keep what you use. Makeup should be thrown away after about six months because of the danger of bacterial growth.

Bedroom

Store seasonal clothing in shallow rolling bins that fit under the bed. If your bed sets close to the floor, you can always purchase sturdy plastic feet that raise it up. A bed skirt will hide items from view while keeping them easily accessible.

Jewelry can be stored in jewelry boxes and placed in dresser drawers, but you can also hang necklaces and bracelets from hooks or pegs on the wall. A tie rack attached to a wall of your closet can organize your jewelry neatly and accessibly, while keeping them out of the way.

The closet floor is often underused, but it makes a great place to store shoes and seasonal clothing in bins.

Office

It is best to declutter your office just like you would your house. Get rid of things you don't use and scan in paperwork for which you do not need originals.

Separate your office into zones, based on what kind of work is performed in that area. Use your computer at a computer station; sort paperwork on a desk, table, or credenza; file paperwork neatly away in binders on shelves or in file cabinets; store office supplies in closets. Label everything in your office, from the inbox, to the contents of your filing cabinet, to items in your supply closet. This will make it much easier to find things and notice when items need replenishing.

Keep a meeting folder and separate folders for each coworker you interact with on a regular basis. Place everything you need for meetings in the meeting folder and any notes pertaining to communication with coworkers in their folders. This type of organization will make you less likely to lose items or to forget to discuss important matters.

I file things I need to read in a box on a bookshelf, so I don't lose them. I also make up a "to do" list every night before I leave the office. A dry erase board on the wall does the trick. The next day, as I complete a task, I just erase it from the board.

Car

My car was terribly disorganized until I started using some storage units I got for a buck at a dollar store. A large beauty bag holds small toys for kids or paperwork you need to keep in your car; it's perfect because it fits in your glove box. A pocket organizer from the dollar store will also work well.

If you have little kids, hook a backpack containing wipes, toys and snacks for each child onto the back of the front seat. Keep a wicker basket or plastic bin in the trunk with bottles of water, emergency flares, flashlights, a first aid kit, high-energy snacks, and blankets.

Use a plastic cereal dispenser as a garbage container; it will fit easily in tight places. Catch a plastic grocery bag over the lip and snap on the top. Flip open the large circular spout to put trash in and when it is full just remove the lid and replace the grocery bag.

Organizing Your Life

Organizing your life is just as important as organizing your home, office, and car. The process is multi-tiered, but once you get the ball rolling, you'll be astounded at the progress you'll make. How you organize your finances will affect your schedule, which in turn will impact how you organize your to-do list, which affects organizing your finances, etc.

Here are ten key tips for organizing your life:

1. **Make the time** – Set aside some time each week to decompress and make out your organizational plan for the days ahead. Taking advantage of this time will equip and prepare you for the challenges of the week to come. You'll go into Monday with a clear, focused mind.

2. **List it out** – Lists (digital or handwritten) are your mapping tool for full organization. Keep track of errands that need to be run, groceries that need to be purchased, calls to be returned, and general to-dos you need to accomplish. Keep your lists in an easily accessible area of your phone, computer, or notebook.

3. **Prep your meals** – Chop, package, and refrigerate or otherwise store all the ingredients for the week's lunches. Freeze what you can in airtight containers and plastic bags so that they last longer. Buy ingredients in bulk whenever you can and plan to use perishables in a timely manner before they go bad.

4. **Clean your house regularly** – A tidy house will encourage you to spend more time at home, instead of spending money by going out to eat. Keeping your house neat and clean will encourage you to enjoy it more. You will also be more likely to invite friends over on the spur of the moment.

5. **Do a digital clean up-** Get rid of excess documents, emails, photos and music to open up space on your computer. Organize what you hold on to in specific folders that are easily accessible. Ensure that your assets are labeled correctly and are easy to track down.

6. **Back up, back up, back up** – Back up your computer data at least once a month, if not more frequently. Utilize free services like Google Drive and iCloud or purchase an external hard drive for your backups.

7. **Set financial goals** – Financial goals are the best way to put more money in the bank. If you set feasible goals for yourself, you'll know exactly what you're working toward with your savings. Put this money in an account that you can't touch. Even if your savings goal is just for "rainy days", you'll feel financially safer knowing that you're protecting your future.

8. **Surround yourself with good friends** – If you spend your time with the right people, you'll feel encouraged to live a much more dynamic and organized life. It might sound harsh, but cutting ties with people who hold you back or put you down is a great tool for organizing your life.

9. **Don't spread yourself too thin** – you have 24 hours in each day, only seven days in a week. Maximize your time to your benefit. Sometimes this will mean saying no to a happy hour or declining a friend's request to hang out. Know your limits and live within them.

    You know your goals and dreams. You also know what you need to do to accomplish them. It almost never comes easily, but those who are the most disciplined and hardest working are usually the ones smiling with the trophy in their hands at the end.

10. **Breathe** – Everything is always fixable. Nothing is so urgent that you don't have time to stop and think things through first. Think of the possible consequences before you act.

Some of these tips will be more immediately applicable to your life than others. Still struggling to get started? Which are most important to you? Start with just one and work to integrate it into your daily life over the next month.

Once you've gotten the hang of this item, add another top-ten tip to your routine. Don't beat yourself up if you have off days; these are all part of the process. Over time you'll appreciate how much better you feel with these habits built into your life. I personally have each area of my life expertly organized; I find it truly amazing how much more efficient, happy and productive you can be when everything in your life is in its proper place!

Chapter 3: Easy Feng Shui Methods

Feng Shui (pronounced *feng shway*) comes to us from the ancient Chinese. It is a method for bringing one's home into harmony with one's environment. Feng Shui and minimalism go hand in hand because both remove clutter from the living area. In minimalism you keep few possessions and those you do have mean much to you. Feng Shui helps you decide where to place your possessions to draw attention to them and to bring the most positive energy into the home.

Both Feng Shui and minimalism promote balance between open space in the home and object placement. It should be noted that even though Feng Shui is an Asian methodology, your home does not have to be decorated in an Asian theme. It works well with any style of decor.

Declutter

One of the ideas behind Feng Shui is that the less clutter you have, the more positive energy there is in a home. This positive energy gives all who live or visit there a sense of freedom.

It is important that the entire house be clutter-free. Do not ignore one area just because it would be hard to declutter. Clutter in even one area will render Feng Shui ineffective.

Placement

In Feng Shui you take control of the way you place your furniture and other objects and thus take control of your life. The command position in any room is a very important place. It usually resides across the room from the door, but at a diagonal angle, so that you can see out the door at all times, but what is going on in the hallway or another room does not directly affect you.

Basic Principles

Feng Shui works under five basic elements which are:

- Wood – symbolized by the color green and indicating renewal

- Fire – symbolized by the color red and triangular shapes as well as light

- Earth – represented by yellow or brown and square shapes

- Metal – symbolized by the color white and round shapes

- Water – represented by the color blue and by water features

In Feng Shui the house is a whole, a living being where each part relates to each other part. Therefore, the garden outside relates to the living room, the living room relates to the bathroom, the bathroom to the bedroom, and so on. Everything is connected.

Attracting Chi

Chi is the positive energy that flows through a house. Its flow should be unimpeded. Sha is negative energy that sometimes enters a home if the principles of Feng Shui are ignored. The best way to avoid sha is to prevent it from ever entering the home.

There are several ways to attract Chi to your home. Improve the curb appeal of your house. Get rid of clutter both outside and inside. Install positive energy-bearing objects near or in the home. Water from a fountain contains positive energy, so a fountain at the front door or inside the home will attract Chi.

Chi is encouraged through learning, so a bookshelf inside the house near the front door will also attract Chi. Wind chimes near a window or door also attract Chi. Other items that Chi is fond of are crystals, mirrors, colors, art, statues or likenesses of Buddha, and certain plants. These objects are wonderful, but it's also important to display items that are meaningful and beautiful to you. In this way, you also adhere to the dictates of minimalism.

Front Door and Outside

A clear path makes it easier for chi to find its way into your house. Placing an attraction object near the door without it being in the way also attracts Chi. The front door is often called the mouth of Chi because this is where it enters. Painting the door a bright color will attract Chi. Use green for wood, red for fire, yellow for earth, white for metal or blue for water. Plants near the door can also attract Chi.

Bedroom

Your bedroom should be a restful place. The command position for the most important piece of furniture in this room, the bed, should be the farthest spot from the door but diagonal to it. A person lying in the bed should be able to see out the door. This encourages strength while sustaining calm. Placing the bed in this area helps you sleep better, it promotes health, and it brings serenity. Since most of us spend a quarter to a third of our lives in bed, this is very important.

Keep electronics out of the bedroom. Certain electronics, like television sets, can emit electric current that can keep you awake. If you must have electronics in the bedroom, keep them at least two feet away from the bed.

Office

Whether your office is at home or in another location, keep your desk in the command position, across from the door and at a slight angle. Never place your back to the door. It is important for chi to flow freely; and in order for this to occur, you must face the door. Facing a solid wall will inhibit your concentration and your creativity.

Plants

Natural and organic items attract a great deal of chi into a home and what better way to do that than to use a plant? Plants represent growth, prosperity, and good luck in Feng Shui. Plants with upward pointing leaves give energy to the environment and those with rounded leaves impart peace.

Green plants purify the air. They take in carbon dioxide and expel oxygen while humans take in oxygen and exhale carbon dioxide. Talk about balance!

Specific plants are important to Feng Shui. Here are just a few of them:

- Bamboo is said to deter bad energy, or sha, and bad spirits. It attracts chi, especially when positioned near wind chimes or water features. It is also said to attract prosperity. You can plant bamboo outside, to the left of your front door if your climate will support it, or opt for odd numbers of lucky bamboo stalks in a pot in a place of prominence indoors. This plant is said to ward off negativity.

- The jade plant sometimes grows into a tree-like configuration. It is a succulent plant and is treated much like a cactus. It does not need a great deal of water but it does need a lot of sunlight. The leaves are leathery and puffy as if they are full of water.

  Jade leaves are oval and resemble coins, so this plant also represents prosperity. In fact, it is often called the money tree. The jade plant should be placed near the entrance of the home to encourage chi. Just be careful if you live in a cold climate that it is protected from winter winds.

- The philodendron has heart shaped leaves and grows like the vine that it is, flourishing in either natural or artificial light. It is reported to lend serenity to a home and make it a welcoming and inviting place. If you train it right, a philodendron will vine up a wall and over doorways.

- The ficus benjamina, or ornamental fig, has pointed oval leaves and grows like a tree. This plant is a great air purifier. It can grow to be fairly large, big enough to divide a room. The ficus is very attractive and can be placed in an area of prominence, preferably near a window that sets across from the front door. A ficus will lose its leaves in a draft, so avoid placing it near heat registers or by doors that are frequently opened.

- The Boston Fern is a frilly plant, beautiful to look at with its lacy leaves. It makes a home feel welcoming. Put it on the porch in summer and in a bright sunny window in the winter.

Feng Shui principles have been in existence for thousands of years, so they have a long history of effectiveness. If you wish to follow a minimalistic lifestyle, you can easily partner with Feng Shui to ensure that your chi is strong and flows freely through your home.

Chapter 4: Mental Release and Meditation Techniques

You may wonder, what do mental release and meditation techniques have to do with minimalism? Actually, they have a great deal in common. The minimalist lifestyle teaches you how to have little and yet thrive in today's society. A need to hold onto material objects may indicate that you have an inability to let go of mental baggage as well.

Minimalists have less to worry about because they have less. Therefore, while you are decluttering your closets and your house, you might as well begin to declutter your emotions and your thoughts. What better way to do this than through emotional release and meditation? The objective of both release and meditation is to clear out all the negative emotions and nagging thoughts that can trap your mind in an unending whirling mass of distraction. As a minimalist, you don't have room for anything that will distract you from living in the moment.

Anyone who has experienced an emotional trauma knows that our minds tend to replay the event over and over. The memory burrows down deep into our brain cells, eventually remaining hidden until something comes along to trigger that memory, and off it goes again, churning through our brain. The emotional pain from this memory blocks energy, or chi, from flowing freely through our bodies.

Emotional Release

Emotional release is a technique that can bring balance to your emotions. It can heal damaged thoughts and ease some of the pain, while helping to eradicate the fear associated with that memory. Meditation is another strategy that can help us take back the control of our emotions and allow us to remain cool, calm and collected. Both require a modicum of practice, but once they are mastered you will be able to clear any energy blockages as they arise.

The following are just a few emotional release methods that are used to clear energy blockages and to allow the Chi to flow freely through both mind and body.

Shifting

Shifting involves changing the way you think about things. It sounds pretty easy, but it takes some practice to actually perform it properly. The point in shifting is to transform negative thoughts into positive ones.

I have a friend whose daughter and 20-month old son were living with the baby's father who provided their only source of income. The father decided he didn't want to be a father any longer and took off for another state. My friend took in her daughter and grandson, but the situation wasn't all that great. My friend's house was quite small, even without the added population. To make things worse, the daughter quickly assumed she had acquired a live-in babysitter, so she felt free to leave the baby with grandma without warning!

My friend sacrificed much of her freedom. She gave up her craft room to her daughter, which meant stuffing everything into the garage and sharing her office with her grandson.

It isn't easy to work when a baby is sleeping in the room. My friend quickly discovered how hard it is to keep up with a 20-month old boy! She knew her house would never be clean again.

This was a negative circumstance for her until she decided she would turn it into a positive one. She chose to be grateful for having more time with her grandson and used the opportunity to bond deeply with him. The smiles and hugs he gave her when she came in from working were worth all the stained carpet and the twisted ankles she suffered when she stumbled over his toys.

My friend soon discovered she could get more work accomplished on the kitchen table than she did in her secluded office. While cooking dinner, she could continue to work. With her office in the kitchen, she no longer felt secluded from the rest of the family.

She was able to shift her attitude from negative things that were happening to her to gratefulness for what was positive about the situation. In essence, she turned her lemons into lemonade.

Visualization

Visualization methods can stop negative thoughts from hanging around in your head. Visualize your brain and see the bad thoughts running through them as rain clouds on a Pac-Man track. Set loose some Pac-Men in your brain and watch them gobble up those rain clouds, leaving only rainbows behind.

Another helpful exercise is to visualize yourself putting all the negative thoughts into a garbage bag. Associate colors and different sounds with these thoughts. Visualize yourself stuffing them into a big black garbage bag and hefting the bag over a steep cliff. Imagine their sounds growing fainter and fainter as the bag falls farther away, until you hear nothing but silence.

Emotional Peace Technique

You don't have to be a minimalist to want emotional peace, but with less to worry about you should be able to attain it easier. Take 10 to 15 minutes and make a list of everything that is negative or that bothers you. Perhaps it seems like you are the only one who can replace an empty toilet paper roll. Maybe you are the only one in the house who knows how to remove a full garbage bag from the trash can (and replace it with a fresh one). You know, we're talking about all those little things that really make your blood boil. Your list can be as simple as leaving the top off the toothpaste or as earth-shattering as a husband who is cheating.

Rate each item you wrote down from one (the least bothersome) to 10 (the most painful). With little things that are not worth your emotional energy, choose to let them go. However, with the major items, you'll want to face them head-on and reach some sort of resolution so that they don't steal the peace from your life in the long term.

Meditation, Prayer and Affirmations

Meditation is a vehicle to achieve inner peace and has been known as such since ancient times. Prayer is communicating with your Source; it can range from the simple, one-word, "Help!" to a short prayer before (and after, if you are a Muslim) meals that thank God for the food, to an intense conversation with your maker. Affirmations are a form of positive self-talk.

Anyone who thinks it is easy to meditate is wrong; it takes practice and discipline. The goal is to block out all the insanity that life offers and only focus on breathing at first. After learning to focus on your breathing, you can progress to visualizations, prayer, or on the repetition of statements of affirmation.

Affirmations

Affirmations are uplifting statements that feed your spirit; they may be considered a form of meditation. For example, in transcendental meditation, the guru gives the person who is meditating a mantra or statement to be repeated; this often is a sort of positive affirmation.

Affirmations help replace your internal negative dialogue with a positive alternative. They can carry you a long ways toward being at peace with yourself and the world around you.

Affirmations are a little easier than what I will call full-blown meditation. They consist of repeating a single phrase or sentence. Affirmations can be spoken anywhere; you can repeat them at your desk, in the shower as part of your morning ritual, or wherever you are. You don't have to sit or stand; you can take any position you like. Your physical posture is completely irrelevant when it comes to affirmations. They don't even require much concentration. You can easily recite them as you drive to work, take a walk, etc.

Affirmations are worded as positive statements. They are realities you have chosen to affirm or truth statements you have selected to guide your life. The affirmation, "I release all my fears and trust in my higher power to protect me" is a guiding statement. It is a promise to yourself that you are choosing trust over fear of the unknown. It also states your confidence that you will be protected and that your needs will be taken care of by a force outside of yourself.

Affirmations can carry you a long way toward inner peace. They are a tool with which to replace negative and destructive thoughts and attitudes with beliefs that build and nourish your life.

The statement of affirmation is a beneficial form of "brainwashing." The idea behind it is that the more often you speak something, the more it becomes real to you. There is nothing wrong with this kind of brainwashing if it helps you become a better person. Here are some affirmations you might find useful in your own life:

- My Source will supply all my needs.//
- I am a spiritual being housed in a physical body.
- I can love myself when I make mistakes.
- I accept each part of myself without judging.
- As I accept myself, so I accept other people, without condemnation.
- I give my love without conditions, expecting nothing in return.
- God's love flows through me and outward toward others.
- I am loving, forgiving, and kind.
- I look for beauty around me.
- I choose to do the right and good thing.
- I see the magic and the miracle in life.
- I have all I need.
- I am growing spiritually.
- I do what I can to ease the troubles of others.
- I acknowledge that there is good in all people, including myself.

I suggest you write your chosen affirmations on index cards. Small three by five inch index cards easily slide into your pocket or your purse for easy access. Take them with you and pull them out for repetition periodically throughout the day. You can also glue a magnetic strip to the back of a card and stick it to your refrigerator at home or a file cabinet at work.

Several times during the day, take a look at your affirmations and speak them out loud if at all possible. Before long, the concepts will become part of your life. You will become what your affirmations suggest, as they become part of your subconscious.

Meditation

Meditation has been linked with spirituality for centuries. Meditation is a means of opening the mind to inner peace.

Many types of meditation exist. You can try most of them by yourself, although some types require personal instruction from a teacher.

J. Krishnamurti, an Indian philosopher and spiritualist, wrote, "Meditation is not a means to an end. It is both the means *and* the end." One effect of meditation is that of calming the whole person. As it brings stillness, it can actually initiate healing and improve physical and emotional health.

Meditation may help you focus on daily tasks and it is able to increase your effectiveness, both at work and at home. If you are frequently called on to make major decisions, you may also benefit; meditation is known to help a person detach emotionally from a situation in order to think clearly and discern the best path to follow. Meditation promotes unwavering focus, which can help keep distractions from derailing your purpose.

In meditation, you experience silence. This includes quieting the inner voice, which is always clamoring for attention. This may not be easy to do at first. You don't just sit down and decide to meditate for 30 minutes unless you've been practicing this and building up to it. As you begin, don't be surprised if you find yourself drifting off into daydreams, falling asleep, or becoming distracted by frustration if you don't succeed in the first couple minutes.

Meditation is a skill; as such, it can be learned. All you need is repeated practice over time. Meditation is difficult at first, but it will be well worth the work. An easy way to start meditating can be found in AudioEntertainment's YouTube Video "[A Beginner's Guide to Meditation~Learn To Meditate in 5 Easy Steps](#)".

Once you get the hang of meditation, you may find yourself calmer and less likely to get angry. In meditation, all bodily functions slow down while your energy increases. Everything from blood flow to breathing becomes slower, until you have reached a sort of balance. I know one person who is able to relax her entire body when meditating. Her pulse decreases to single digits and if you were to raise her arm above her head and let go, it would fall limply to her side.

In meditation, the spirit becomes freer; peacefulness takes over. You can receive communication from spiritual sources, when in meditation. The calm that occurs during meditation is something you can actually carry with you into other life situations.

Transcendental Meditation

One common type of meditation, made famous during the 1960s and '70s by celebrities including the Beatles, is called transcendental meditation. This is an intense form of meditation, patterned after the Hindu practice of Vedanta meditation.

In transcendental meditation, the practitioner sits comfortably and clears the mind of all chatter and clutter by repeating a mantra given by a guru. This mantra may be something as simple as "I am strong, powerful and compassionate". The lotus position is the posture most suited to this type of meditation because it can be sustained for a long time without too much discomfort.

Zen Meditation

Zen or Zazen meditation is another popular form that uses a koan, or a phrase that focuses upon a riddle with no real answer. The theory behind this type of meditation is that the mind will overwhelm itself and stop thinking altogether when an answer cannot be reached. The result is total silence.

This mediation requires the body to sit in a very *un*comfortable position. You sit with your spine straight and your back completely unsupported. After a while the body begins to ache. You are expected to remain in this position without thinking as you pass through the pain onto the other side.

Mindful Meditation

Mindful meditation is a bit easier and is highly popular today. It is derived from the Buddhist meditation practice of Vipassana. In mindful meditation, you focus on being fully present, whether you are on a bus going home or in your bedroom. You allow your mind to wander freely and you observe, without judgment, whatever thoughts surface. The idea here is that the mind will eventually calm itself and will quiet down.

Walking Meditation

When you walk in a quiet place and focus on your walking, you are performing walking meditation. This is sometimes done in a labyrinth, but you can walk anywhere: along a path, on a sidewalk, around a track, or in a parking lot. When your body is in motion it is easier to focus on what it is doing. Pay attention to what each part of your body does to impel you forward.

Other, more challenging forms of meditation include **Qigong**, a healing form of meditation with roots in the martial arts, and **Kundalini yoga**, which has a profound religious underpinning dealing with chakras and the coiling snake of the spine.

Think of meditation as a way to let off steam from everyday life. Use it as a tool to calm your mind while increasing your spiritual awareness. Meditation can help you think clearly, move more intentionally, and live more calmly.

Emotional Relaxation

Emotional release techniques often use meditation as a vehicle to achieve relaxation. One is the **Meditation Relaxation Technique**, a deep form of relaxation that can melt stress away. It slows down the breath rate and blood flow and lowers the blood pressure.

We all have a tiny nut-like portion of our brain called the amygdala, which controls what is called the "fight or flight" response. When we are confronted with a problem or our brain decides we are in danger, the amygdala kicks in and we either fight the problem or we flee from it.

Emotions can trigger this fight-or-flight response; when this happens, it is good to have practiced meditation relaxation. The meditation relaxation technique helps you control your impulses and drop into a deep form of relaxation, so that you don't react without first analyzing the situation. In many cases the fight-or-flight response turns out to be unnecessary, so this technique may well save you from undue stress and later embarrassment.

To begin meditation relaxation, you sit or lie comfortably in an area where you will not be disturbed. Close your eyes and begin by turning your awareness toward the top of your head. Feel your forehead muscles relax. Then move on to your cheeks and your chin. After you feel these muscles relax, move on to your neck, your shoulders, then your upper back and your collarbone area.

Shift your awareness gradually down each arm to the fingers, relaxing every muscle group as you go. Then move down the trunk of your body, both front and back. Give special attention to your belly, then move your attention around to your lower back, following your mind's eyes over your relaxing hips, buttocks, thighs and on down your legs to your feet bones and the muscles of your toes.

Progressive Muscle Relaxation

If any part of your body resists your command to relax, tighten those muscles for a few seconds and then let them release. This tense-and-relax strategy is another emotional release technique called progressive muscle relaxation. It takes a lot of practice to isolate specific muscle groups for tensing and release. It is often a challenge to keep your head relaxed while you tense other muscles on the way to relaxing your feet. You will need a certain level of concentration for this exercise, but it will be facilitated as you learn to ignore everything except what your body is feeling at the moment.

Ommm

While you are relaxing each muscle in your body, keep breathing steadily in and out. If it helps, you can speak a sound when breathing out. Believe it or not, "Ommm" is the perfect word. It means nothing and it can be sustained as you breathe out. The vibrations created by this sound can help your muscles relax.

Take about 20 minutes to complete this activity. Avoid setting an alarm; when it goes off your body will instinctively tense up, destroying all you have accomplished! Instead, peek occasionally at a clock placed nearby.

Most of us have a conversation going on in our heads at all times. This is called the inner voice. The object of meditation is to stop that little voice and give it a rest. When your meditation time is up, stay in position for a few minutes, while you ease your eyes open and let your other senses wake up to the outside world.

Diaphragmatic Breathing

Deep breathing is another meditation technique that is quite helpful for emotional release. Singers breathe differently than most people. A trained vocalist breathes in by extending the diaphragm, a layer of muscles directly beneath the lungs. When the diaphragm expands, it enlarges the lungs from the bottom, allowing them to fill with air. When many people consciously breathe in, their shoulders raise, but this is not true for singers. Their shoulders remain lowered and the stomach expands when breathing in. When exhaling, the shoulders remain in place while the stomach goes in as the diaphragm contracts. This pushes the air out of the lungs more efficiently.

To experience diaphragmatic breathing, lie on your back on a bed or on the floor and place a hardback book on your stomach. Breathe in and watch the book rise. Breathe out and watch it move down. Don't breathe too quickly or you can hyperventilate. Once you get the idea of how to breathe with a singer's breath, stand up and put one hand on your stomach and one behind your back. Be careful to keep your shoulders relaxed.

Breathe in and feel your hands move apart. Then exhale and feel them move closer together. Once you get the hang of breathing this way, sit in a comfortable position and concentrate on your breath, breathing in and out slowly about five times at first. Breathe naturally. Work your way up to 10 or 20 breaths. Counting breaths is one type of meditation.

Once you are proficient at these meditation techniques, the emotional relaxation kicks in. When you are presented with a problem that triggers your emotions, start controlled breathing or other relaxation techniques. You can perform them standing or seated, once you understand how they work. This will help you calm down and respond rationally, without undue interference from your emotions.

Forgive

Being able to forgive others and yourself is a great way to achieve mental release. When you hold things inside, they just stew in there, waiting to come out in the form of negative expressions.

It is hard to forgive someone if you don't have all the facts, so do what you can to gain insight into the reason behind the other person's action. Understanding what influences affected your opponent makes it possible for you to empathize with the person as a human, especially if it is not within the realm of her normal behavior. There may be extenuating circumstances that precipitated the words or actions. The offender may not be aware of his betrayal or it may have been deliberate. Until you understand all the facts of the situation, it is difficult to forgive. Learning and understanding is an integral part of the process.

We need explanations. It is human nature to seek understanding. Even if the explanation isn't what we desire to hear, we still need it in order to move forward. Was the betrayal a form of retribution for something we did? Was it a mean-spirited jab or just happenstance? This information can help start the process of forgiveness. We also need it in order to learn from a situation so that it won't happen again.

The Offense Against Carolyn

Carolyn wanted to be Sunday school superintendent at church. She had been involved in teaching Sunday School for years. She helped with all the Christmas pageants, participated in vacation Bible school, and even gave input into the Sunday school curriculum. The day finally came when the superintendent relinquished her position, and the board of directors appointed someone else to take her place, someone much less experienced than Carolyn.

Carolyn was deeply hurt. She suspected that the board president did not like her and she felt betrayed and belittled. No one else did so much for the Sunday School as Carolyn. She felt that not only should she have been appointed, but her friends should have stood up for her! To make things worse, the woman they appointed to the post didn't even have any children!

Carolyn didn't know exactly why she was passed over for the position, but she felt angry and became somewhat vindictive. Before her root of bitterness did any real damage however, she chose to seek out a board member and asked why she had been turned down.

It turned out that Carolyn actually *was* considered for the position, but because she had two jobs, was raising two teenagers and a grandchild, and her husband was sick, the board thought she had her hands too full to take on any more. They didn't want to burden her further. Instead of rejecting her, the board held her in high respect. There was no animosity there, just concern for her welfare.

Chastened by their kindness, it was easy for her to forgive the board and accept their decision. As a result, she and the president of the board became fast friends. Understanding and learning "the rest of the story" had paved the way for forgiveness.

Repeat Offenders

When Bishop T. D. Jakes was asked how to forgive someone who repeatedly hurts you, he came up with an interesting analogy. In a conversation with Oprah, he described people who have limited capacity for good as pint people. Those with greater stores he called gallon people. He urged us to seek to understand why certain people act the way they do, and to adjust our expectations according to their capacities. While we'll always come up against pint people, said Jakes, we should strive to surround ourselves with gallon people. Check out his explanation in the YouTube video, Bishop T.D. Jakes on How to Forgive a Repeat Offender, by OWN TV.

Turn Pain into Gain

When you are betrayed, you may feel you are being tested. Buddhists believe that those who have the most adversity in life are much closer to enlightenment than those with an easier life. They view difficulties as tests that teach. Is your current difficulty due to your need to learn patience? When you suffer hard times, look for what strengths you may develop as a result of your experiences.

Dwayne's Story

Dwayne was pretty useless around the house. He was lost in the kitchen, had no idea how to do laundry, and never even paid his bills on time. His wife did all that and took care of the kids as well. She apparently had enough at one point, however, because she left Dwayne and the kids for a younger man.

It was a terrible betrayal, but because of it Dwayne learned many things. He learned how to cook and clean. He learned to pay the bills, and built new relationships with his kids. Forgiving his ex-wife was difficult but after a while, it wasn't so hard. He actually decided to thank her and the guy who lured her away, because of all the things he had subsequently gained. This painful betrayal had enrolled Dwayne in a learning experience that greatly enriched his life in the long run.

We learn from the past, so take past experiences and learn from them. Often, we can apply what we have learned to new situations. Experience can shine a new light on matters, helping us resolve issues more quickly. Awareness of our own struggles can enhance our ability to forgive others and to be more patient with their struggles.

Ask for Advice

Learn from someone who has been in a similar circumstance. You could talk to friends who have suffered like Dwayne, to see how they let go of the anger and pain of betrayal. They may be able to shed new light on your situation that helps you offer forgiveness to the person who hurt you. You can also hire a life coach or a counselor, talk to a friend, read a book, or research online. However you accomplish it, reach out for help in order to avoid getting stuck in bitter unforgiveness.

Define Forgiveness

Do a little research about forgiveness and write down some quotes and a definition on index cards. Stick these cards on your refrigerator where you can see them every day. Understanding and learning about forgiveness helps us to forgive.

Counseling

Seek counseling if you just can't forgive someone. A therapist is trained to help you to understand the problem and why you need it resolved, both for yourself and for the offender.

Personal Growth Expert, Noah Hammond, produced a YouTube video called How To Forgive Someone Quickly And Easily. It teaches you forgiveness principles, such as understanding that everyone does the best they can with the tools they have, why people do things that hurt others, and why forgiveness has to start from within.

Learning to forgive is a difficult lesson. It takes time, but the best thing about it is that it gets easier with knowledge, understanding and practice.

One of the best ways to heal emotions and get rid of emotional baggage is to forgive. Holding on to grudges and resentments will clutter your mind with junk. Just like you clean your closet, you can clean out grudges and be free again.

Forgiveness does not undo the past. You can forgive someone and still be cautious with him, to prevent whatever happened from happening again. Forgiving someone just frees you from anger. It is a method to help you let go, just like you let go of those 20 spatulas you were hanging onto in the kitchen.

Here are some steps to forgiveness:

1. Commit to letting go. Tell yourself now is the time. Remind yourself that holding on to your resentment is not doing anyone any good.

2. Understand that you do have a choice. You do not have to let go if you don't want to. However, since you have let go of so much in your life already, it is probably a good idea to get rid of this baggage, too.

3. Practice empathy. Put yourself in the offending person's shoes. Why did she do what she did? Was it just to cause you pain? Could his actions have been unintentional?

4. Understand your responsibility in the situation. What did you do to precipitate the injury?

5. Evaluate the relationship. Would your life be better without her? Do you have little choice because you're living with him? Is this relationship important enough to hold on to? Is it salvageable?

6. Throw away your pain and anger. Put it in a bag and throw it over a cliff.

7. Allow peace to enter. Relax or meditate and let peace enter your heart while you visualize the person who hurt you.

8. Feel compassion. It is possible this person is also unhappy with the situation. Let yourself feel compassion toward the one who wronged you.

Gratitude

Thankfulness for what you have is a big emotional healer. If you've pared down your possessions when you organized and decluttered, you can be grateful for what you still have. You can be grateful for your life, health, friends, family, pets and other things in your life.

When negative thoughts come into view, use your mind-shifting abilities and transform them into thoughts of gratitude. Then find a way to express your gratitude. The act of expression will reinforce this way of thinking. As you repeatedly express your gratitude, you will be forming a habit of gratefulness.

Here are 20 ways you can express your gratitude:

1. Write Gratitude Letters. You can write letters to the people in your life who have meant something to you. You may wish to simply thank them for their presence in your life, or for the benefits that their advice or support have given you.

I have found it beneficial to write gratitude letters to people with whom I haven't had particularly great dealings, as a reminder that each person was sent into my life for a purpose. Every person I encounter is given to me so that I can learn something new. That truth alone is very empowering. By being grateful to others for the lessons learned, we can wipe away the pain we have experienced.

2. Cultivate the gift of amazement. "*At least once a day, stop long enough to allow yourself to be truly amazed by a tree, or a flower, or the sunlight dancing on land or sea. That is the sacred space, the place within us where we are witness to the ongoing miracles of life. And the more we are open to truly seeing them around us, the more we are able to truly feel them within us. Miracles are everywhere, all the time, waiting to be plucked by our awareness into the makings of a happy life.*" (Marianne Williamson, Facebook, June 15, 2014)

3. Express your gratitude in person. This one can be a little tough to start with, but start by thanking staff in the stores you visit for their service. Thank the person on the other end of the telephone when you call about your gas bill. Even if you are unhappy with the service the company has provided, these people are doing their best, so they deserve our thanks for putting up with terrible wages and unpleasant working conditions to do a soul-destroying job where all they ever hear is complaints. Make their day; thank them for their service.

    Tell your best friends why you are so happy they are part of your life. Tell your partner you appreciate him even when he is doing something as mundane as the dishes! Trust me, once you start doing this you will find people itching to do even more for you. We all just love to be appreciated.

4. Take "Mental Gratitude Pictures." Prasanna is legally blind, and though this has caused no end of struggles, it has taught him to value every day and to seize the moment whenever possible. I am currently trying to use his method in my daily practice. It is a rather beautiful one, I think.

    "*I take what I call 'mental gratitude pictures' and write about these pictures in my gratitude journal*", he says. "*Usually, this process involves me 1) pausing; 2) taking notice of a particular moment, image, or detail around me; 3) taking a deep breath; 4) closing my eyes; and 5) envisioning the moment, image, or detail in my mind.*" (Huffington Post, July 17, 2014)

5. Express your gratitude in art. This is one for the creative among you. If you have artistic leanings of any kind – musical, literary, fine art, photography, pottery – you can make a small gift to say thank you. This

is all the more appreciated when it's not expected, so prepare an appropriate thank you give and present it out of the blue.

You can also use your artistic capabilities to express your gratitude in your journal. Cut out, draw, or take pictures of the things you are grateful for and make a collage.

6. Practice spiral gratefulness writing. Tony Robbins of The "Unlimited Power" audio series likes to describe his gratefulness in an outward spiral progression beginning with himself. I used this method when I first began my gratefulness practice and it is one I highly recommend. .

   The process is lovely and simple. Start with yourself in the center and write outward in a spiral. Tony uses a set order – one I think is most apt – that saves the least important things until last.

   Start by writing what you are grateful for in yourself, including both physical and mental attributes. Next include the people in your life, writing the physical and mental attributes that you most admire. Following this, write about your pets, your career, your hobbies, and the things you own.

   Here is an example of the Tony Robbins technique: "I am grateful for my heart, my knowledge and skills. I am grateful for my strong body and quick mind. I am grateful for my full hair and my excellent vision. I am grateful for my friends and their loving support of me in whatever I do. I am grateful for my family, that they are strong and healthy. I am grateful for my pets, that they give me love so unconditionally. I am grateful for my career as a writer and the wonderful people who buy my books. I am grateful for my wonderful home and my wonderful possessions that make my life easier and brighter."

7. Make a gratitude date. Set aside a specific time to sit down with your partner or your family and talk about all the things that you are all thankful for. We are supposed to do this on Thanksgiving, but how many of us just jump right into the turkey and dressing, the parade and the football, without thinking about what are grateful for?

   In my way of thinking, gratefulness shouldn't be limited to one day a year. I highly recommend setting aside regular times to speak your gratitude to each other as a family and making this a part of your life as members of that family unit. It will strengthen the bonds between you.

8. Journal your gratefulness. Write down three to five things you are grateful for each night before you go to bed.

9. Devote a specific time each day to gratitude. It could be when you first get up, when you go to bed, before you eat, or when you get home from work. This practice only takes a few minutes, but can make a huge difference in how you view your day.

10. Use Social Media. I find it keeps me focused on gratitude to post regularly on social media. I made a public commitment to post what I'm grateful for on a daily basis for a month.

    I post three things first thing in the morning, three at lunchtime, and then a further three just before I go to bed. I try to post at least one photograph a day, ideally one I have taken on my walk, to illustrate my thankfulness. This is a simple method, but I am finding it really is having an impact.

11. Try to view your day from a place of gratitude. Allow yourself to be amazed by the goodness you usually take for granted. Give yourself a moment to express your gratefulness for what you notice.

12. Practice converting every negative <u>attitude</u> to a positive one. For example, let's say you dread spending all day in a conference room. Try reversing this negative attitude by looking around you and finding something positive. Perhaps the person leading the meeting is positive and upbeat. Maybe there is a great view from a window. Maybe you are sitting next to your favorite person in the office. You can even feel grateful that your coffee is hot and tasty.

13. Gratitude requires humility, but it can be difficult to humble ourselves to acknowledge the contributions of others. Make a conscious effort to thank someone who is younger or poorer than you for ways they have benefitted your life.

14. Give yourself at least one compliment a day, and compliment at least one other person. This can be someone you love, or even a complete stranger. Your compliment doesn't have to be anything huge; it can be a simple as, "That top you're wearing today really flatters you" to yourself in the mirror; or a "Thanks so much; that was lovely" to the waitress who collects your used coffee cup.

15. Try to look at things that go wrong as learning opportunities. Rather than bemoaning the painful reality, try to figure out what you can carry forward from the experience, and choose to be grateful for a lesson you will not forget.

16. Try to take a day, just one day, where you do not moan, complain, criticize, or gossip about others. This can be a difficult challenge, but take note of how often you find yourself about to do these things. Don't beat yourself

up if you slip occasionally; you are only human after all! You will be amazed at how much energy and time you save by cutting out these non-productive negative actions and thoughts.

17. If someone calls you on the telephone, try to sound genuinely pleased that they have called. People can hear it in your voice when you're harried, harassed, and don't really want to talk. We all have times when things are hectic, but it costs nothing to answer the phone with a bright and breezy, "How lovely to hear your voice; I am so glad you called, but things are a little manic right now. Is it okay if I call you back in a few minutes?"

18. Get involved with a cause that matters to you. Donate money, time or your skills. You will gain an even greater appreciation for the work that others do. You will appreciate how great your life is in comparison with other peoples' experiences. Charities are always appreciative of donors and volunteers; they know they cannot function without them, so volunteering is a wonderful way to feel valued, needed, and appreciated.

19. Mark your anniversaries and birthdays with a letter of gratefulness for the past and expectation for the future. This is a wonderful practice, because it requires reflection on the past year and encourages a positive outlook on the future. Write a letter full of excitement and hope for how the year ahead will pan out. Seal the letter in an envelope and, when when you get to the next year, open it up to see how you fared in comparison!

20. Learn to appreciate a force bigger than yourself. People who have faith in God, the Universe, or some greater Force, often see the world through the eyes of gratitude. The next time you see a beautiful flower, or feel a drop of rain or a snowflake settle on your face, lift you head and heart up to your Source and offer thanks for the gift of this world filled with beauty. For more advanced information on this topic, be sure to check out my enlightened book on Spirituality.

Hypnosis

Hypnosis can help with difficult emotions that resist being released. The practice helps you relax your subconscious mind, rendering it highly responsive to suggestions that will help you rid yourself of negative emotions and harmful thoughts. Always enlist the help of a certified hypnotist who knows exactly why you are seeking this treatment.

Tapping

This method of emotional release is also called Emotional Freedom Technique or EFT. You don't need any special equipment, just your fingers. Tapping works on the concept that emotion disrupts the energy, or chi, in the body and the flow needs to be balanced in order for your emotions to be freed.

There are several meridians on the body and you tap five to seven times on each of them in order to balance the chi. This technique was developed by psychologist Roger Callahan. One of his patients was so severely afraid of water that she could not pass by a lake without great anxiety. He prescribed tapping on specific meridians to stop the patient's fear. Later on, Gary Craig discovered that tapping on all of the meridians, worked just as effectively, and EFT was born.

How To Use EFT

The first step is to focus on the negative issue that is affecting your life. You will want to speak aloud a statement that expresses the issue. For example, if you are anxious about going to a job interview you might say, "I probably won't get this job because I have little experience in this field." Next, you will turn your fear statement into a positive, affirming focus statement. In this case the focus statement could be, "Even though I feel anxious about this interview, I accept myself and know that I have the abilities needed to do this job." Rate your anxiety on a 10-point scale, with 10 being the highest and one being the lowest.

Tap on your body using multiple fingers, as if you were testing a ripe melon. Tap each area five to seven times. Repeat your focus statement as you begin each area. Here are the instruction for tapping on each area of your body:

- Outer edge of hand – Tap one hand on the outer edge with all five fingers. This is the area that would take the hit if you were doing a karate chop.

- Head – Tap the center of the crown of the head with four fingers.

- Eyebrow – Tap the inner edges near the bridge of your nose with two fingers.

- Side of eyes – Tap the hard area between the eye and the temple with two fingers.

- Under the eye – Tap the hard area between the cheekbone and the eye, right under the pupil of the eye, with two fingers.

- Under the nose – Tap the area under the nose and above the lip right under the nose with two fingers.

- Chin – Tap under the lower lip on the chin with four fingers.

- Collarbone – Tap below the hard ridge of the collar bone on both sides with four fingers.

- Underarm – Tap the armpit with four fingers and take a deep breath.

Rate your anxiety again from 10 to 1. If your anxiety can be downgraded you can stop, but if it has not gone down, begin the process with the top of the head and then the side of the hand again. Many people find that this will release emotions by the time they get back to the starting point again.

Hopefully, some of these mental release techniques and forms of meditation will help you to get rid of any clutter in your mind and open you up to greater peace and joy. Minimizing your emotional baggage makes room for you to move from survival mode to truly living and that's what minimalism is all about

Chapter 5: Secrets to Healthy and Happy Relationships

Minimalism is not limited to the physical items that surround you. Emotion, as we saw in the previous chapter, is one example of a non-physical entity that ties in with minimalism. Managing relationships is another.

A simple, happier life is the aim of the minimalist. Sometimes our relationships just don't fit in with that "happier" label. These people bring stress and anger into our lives; they often seem to bring out the worst in us. It isn't that these people are just jerks, although that may be the case. You may still really care about them.

You are not obligated to keep anyone in your life if you are doing harm to them or they are consistently harming you. Even family. Although you are kind of stuck with family, you can minimize your exposure to the most toxic individuals.

I am calling for you to declutter the toxic relationships, the ones that don't work, and the friendships you don't need in order to have a happy life. Clear them away, in order to have more time for the good relationships, the ones that bring you joy.

How to Tell if a Relationship is Toxic

Here are some red flags that may indicate you have a toxic relationship with someone:

1. You want to change the other person – You can't change people. You have no power to make them stop doing things that exasperate you. Either accept the person as he is, or choose to distance yourself from the things that bug you.

2. Your body reacts negatively. If you feel uncomfortable or tense around the other person, that is a big danger signal. If you feel physically and emotionally weary when faced with the prospect of time together, it's a clear sign the something is not right with the relationship.

3. You feel like you are losing yourself, or you are not able to fully be yourself when you are together. A healthy friendship should encourage you to be *more* yourself, not less.

4. Your "No" is not heard. This is the most basic test of a relationship. If you do not have the freedom to say no to anything that is proposed, you are not in a relationship but a malevolent dictatorship. Flee for your life!

5. You can't do anything right. If you feel like you are constantly walking on eggshells around him, if it seems like everything you do upsets her, you are in a toxic relationship.

6. The relationship is a one-way street. Any friendship is a matter of give and take, of mutually shared life. If you find that you are always giving, but never receiving in return, it is time to re-evaluate the relationship. Talk things over with your friend and see if you can come to a more equitable division of responsibilities in the relationship.

Building Intentional Friendships

Make a list of qualities you value in a friendship or intimate relationship. Evaluate your friendships in light of these qualities and decide if you want to keep the friendships as is, or if you choose to distance yourself.

Think about your friends. If you let a relationship go entirely, how will you feel? Will you miss her? Will your life be better or worse without him? Use these questions to help you decide how tightly you want to hold on to your friendships.

Relationships should be intentional, but it should not be like pulling teeth to keep a relationship current. If you find that you are always the one to initiate connections, it is time to weigh the importance of the friendship against the cost of keeping in touch.

Loneliness

There are worse things than being alone. It is difficult to let go of someone we are attached to, even if the relationship is less than ideal. If we are not content with being ourselves, the tendency is to glom onto the nearest person, out of fear of being alone.

My cousin was in her early fifties when she met up with a very handsome and debonair man 10 years her junior. They dated for a long time, but she never seemed happy. She would go fishing with him because he loved to go fishing. She went to hockey games with him because he loved hockey. She accompanied him to country music concerts even though she deplored country music.

She loved the opera and theater but always found someone else to go with her to those venues. He never went and when I asked why, she replied that he hated opera and would rather watch TV than a play. Yet, he expected her to go to everything he liked, whether she liked it or not.

I asked my cousin if she loved this man; after a moment of hesitation, she replied that yes, she did. I asked why she stayed in the relationship when she was the only one giving. She said she was afraid of being alone. She was older and thought nobody else would be interested in her. Isn't that a sad way to live?

In the end, she got fed up with the man and booted him out. About three months later she met an older gentleman who shared her love for museums, opera and the theater. They married and couldn't be happier. She told me it was better to enjoy life with an older man who believed in give and take than to suffer in a relationship with an extremely attractive selfish young jerk.

Ending a Toxic Friendship

I had a high school friend who left shortly after we graduated and only recently moved back to town. We started going out to eat occasionally and attended some concerts and sporting events, like we did when we were younger. We had kept in touch all those years while he lived elsewhere and it was very exciting when he returned home.

I thought we could just pick up where we had left off in our friendship, but I soon discovered he had changed – well, we had both changed. Every time we got together, we would bicker and disagree. Everything I said was wrong. I started agreeing with him just to keep peace in the relationship. I loved him as a brother, but this relationship was turning toxic.

It isn't easy to end a friendship after many years. I could have just stopped answering his calls, I could have avoided him around town and I could have just become cold and nasty. Yet, out of respect for him, I couldn't be nasty about it.

The best way to end a toxic relationship is in person. I invited him to my house when no one else would be there. We sat down over some refreshments and I told him the truth. I said that our constant bickering was harming me. We were being destructive to each other by continuing to see each other and I thought we should end the friendship.

He did not realize that I had been upset when we were together. He had viewed our bickering as two competitive personalities interacting I asked if he enjoyed himself when we were together. After thinking for a moment, he said no, recalling how he would go home after our visits and complain about me to his wife. In the end, we chose not to end our friendship entirely, but to back off and only visit occasionally.

Never just email or text someone that you want to end a relationship. Unless your safety is threatened, an in-person talk is the kindest way to go about it. The other person may get upset and cry; they might even scream at you, but it is best to end a toxic relationship. This holds true even if you aren't pursuing minimalism.

Stay True To Good Friends

It is important to nurture your healthy friendships. Here are a few ways to keep a relationship alive, whether as friends or lovers:

- **Relive the past.** Go to a vacation spot where you and your friend or lover had a great time in the past. As a kid, my best friend's family and mine used to go together to "The Lake" and rent a cabin for a week. If this is your fond memory, see if that cabin still rents out. Arrange for you and your friend to take your families there once again.

- **Clarify your expectations**. Make sure your friend or lover knows what you want in the relationship. I don't know why, but we tend to be afraid to tell another person exactly what we want in a relationship. It would be so much easier if we talked about this. Wouldn't misunderstandings be prevented if everybody were on the same page? Don't assume you know what your friend or lover wants. Ask, and then arrange your expectations accordingly, so no one is disappointed or surprised.

- **Know the other person well.** Do you know what is your best friend's favorite color? Do you know your lover's favorite food? Make it a point to discover the intricacies that make your friend or lover who they are.

- **Become a positive conversationalist**. Communication is important in any relationship. Instead of asking, "How was your day?" add some creativity and ask, "What made you the happiest today?" or "what challenged you the most today?" You will receive more interesting responses by connecting with your friend's experiences.

- **Keep in contact**. Check in with friends at least once a week and touch base with close family members others every day or so. Send emails or texts thanking friends for specific kindnesses. Put notes in a lunch box. Plan a date night or establish a regularly scheduled time to phone and touch base.

- **Use creativity to keep things interesting**. Dinner and a movie is fun, but kick it up a notch once in a while by developing a scavenger hunt at a local museum. Go hiking in a forest, go deep sea fishing, or take a cooking lesson together from a famous chef.

- **Don't agree if it's just to keep the peace**. Sometimes we just don't see eye to eye. An explanation can quell sore emotions and open discussion can help you understand where the other person is coming from. You may still not agree, but at least you know where each other stands.

- **Apologize when you are wrong**. An apology can go a long way to heal a wounded relationship. We all sometimes wrong people we care about. Humble yourself and do what you can to make things right again.

- **Support is key**. Relationships are a two-way street. You support your friend or lover and they support you. If a friend is participating in a walk for cancer in memory of a family member who died of the disease, you walk too; if you can't walk, at least contribute to the fund.

   If a friend is having a hard time with his job, listen to his problems; just listen and empathize. Only offer advice if it is requested.

- **Love instead of controlling**. A true friendship is a free meeting of equals. Control is not even in the picture. Give your love freely, without demanding to shape your friend's response. Receive your friend's love, accepting it without condition.

- **Pick friends over money.** Money alone cannot bring you happiness; only rich friendships can do this. Research finds that those who have multiple friends are likely to be 70% happier on average than those who don't. You don't need hundreds of friends either, just a handful of really strong ones.

- **Tell your loved ones that you love them.** The strongest relationships are built upon a foundation of mutual appreciation. Don't fear being vulnerable; after all, this is someone you trust. Speak your appreciation. Say it out loud, because no matter how close they are, your friends cannot read your mind. Hearing how you feel, in your voice, is the most powerful way to communicate.

   Successful relationships are continuously built and nurtured. Watch the YouTube video, An Experiment in Gratitude by SoulPancake, to be inspired by the effects of gratitude in action.

- **Don't compare your relationships to those of others**. Remember, every relationship is different. The relationships you have with your parents, siblings, friends, and significant others are unique to your life. Appreciate what you have in your own relationships! You will find yourself much more satisfied as you celebrate what you have.

- **Find common interests with your loved ones.** Sharing common interests with friends can increase your happiness. What's better than sharing a fun experience with the people that you love? Whether you both enjoy karaoke, watching a game, biking, or just conversing, these activities are infinitely more interesting when you share the experience together.

- **Laugh together.** I am sure you have heard that "laughter is the best medicine." Well, it just might be! Research affirms that many adults link humor with happiness. This is even more effective when it is shared. Read joke books together. Share jokes with your loved one and spread the laughter! With enough practice, people will love to be around you and you'll feel great knowing that you can brighten the lives of others. If you really want to have a good time, check out my book: <u>Laughter and Humor Therapy</u>.

- **Spend time with family.** In today's fast-paced world, it can be challenging to make time for family. However, as your closest ties, they should be high on your priority list. Spending time with your family is essential to sustain healthy relationships.

    Time with your family can be enjoyable, too. Share laughter, get to know each other better, relive fond memories and listen to their concerns. You want your family to be there for you, so don't forget to be there for your family.

    Research shows that spending time with your family can strengthen the relationships between parents and children. Research also affirms that the better your relationships are with those who are closest, the happier you are likely to feel.

- **Address loved ones when they annoy you.** We're talking about vulnerability again, but vulnerability is essential in a healthy relationship. Don't give in to the temptation to bow to things that make you uncomfortable. If you agree with others just to please them, you are giving up a part of who you are. It is much better to calmly address your loved one, explain what is upsetting you, and try to work out a solution. Odds are, your friend had no idea what was bothering you and will be eager to make things right.

    Communication is the key to happiness. Research shows that those who believe they can freely raise concerns with their loved ones are 40% more likely to be happy.

- **Don't criticize harshly.** When you harshly criticize a loved one, it can rock their feelings as well as yours. People rely on their closest friends for support. Harsh criticism can leave deep wounds.

    Although it can be tempting to criticize, accept your loved ones for who they are and think about their positive traits. In a situation where you truly feel that you have to say something, try to come across as gently and as loving as possible. Explain how you feel when the other person does what irritates you, and then listen to their reply.

- **Make others feel needed.** Making others feel needed is another win-win situation. You love it when people make you feel needed, right? Do the same for somebody else. When a person feels important, it often motivates him to live at his best.

    Yes, once again, you become vulnerable when you reveal your weakness, but who better to trust than a proven friend? Plus, when you let somebody else feel needed, it can help you feel good about yourself, knowing that you've made a difference in someone's life.

Good friends are hard to find, so do what you can to protect and nurture your friendships. A good relationship with relatives is like gold. Harmony in a family keeps you feeling safe and secure without the need for external trappings. Nurturing great relationships with your friends and loved ones is one way to live a happier and a simpler life.

Chapter 6: Minimalism Techniques with Technology

Technology can be a minimalist's friend. It can save you a lot of room when you store photos, CDs, DVDs, books, magazines or other valuable information digitally. It can also save you time and aggravation by making these items more immediately accessible.

My photos that were lying around gathering dust were easily scanned and went from three large boxes to one small flash drive backed up on the cloud. The thousands of CDs I had collected for years were ripped onto my computer. I never buy CDs anymore; I just download the music. No muss, no fuss.

The digital age is perfect for a minimalist, even though it may involve using several devices. I own a Kindle, an iPod, a computer, and a smartphone, but this is just four small items, as opposed to my previous boxes upon boxes. My pictures and music are now much more accessible; they are sharable across my digital systems and I can find whatever I need by typing in a simple search phrase.

Technology helps the minimalist stay organized and it can assist them in day-to-day affairs as well.

Special Software

I can't recommend enough getting a program like OneNote or EverNote! A friend told me about OneNote 16 months ago and I ignored her advice for about four months. I finally got around to looking into it and all I can say is, "**WOW!**" This program has been life changing. I have been using OneNote for more than a year now and it has allowed me to set up my life like a peak performance mastermind genius! If used properly, you can organize so much on this system! OneNote automatically saves things instantly; you can store links to websites and YouTube videos; you can easily create a digital journal just by organizing entries according to month; you can compartmentalize your life with separate sections dedicated to personal life and business; you can subdivide sections endlessly, giving you immediate access to each part of your life.

I put everything on OneNote and backed it up online, but you can also back up your information on an external hard drive. I would highly recommend a program like this to easily organize almost every aspect of your digital life.

Calendars

I don't keep a paper calendar anymore. Instead, I keep one on my computer and smartphone that sync together and also mesh with the calendars of other family members. Just a single touch brings up my fully marked calendar. My calendar lets me know in advance when I have a meeting scheduled so I no longer miss appointments. Storing my calendar on multiple devices prevents loss in the event that any one device breaks or is stolen.

Photos

Storing your photos on a flash drive, an external hard drive, on your computer, or on the cloud is quite simple. You can scan and store your photos yourself, or you can send them to a service that will scan the images for you. Scanning items yourself does take time, but it will save you some money if funds are tight.

I also recommend saving your photos on the cloud, to avoid losing them. After scanning them, you can always give the paper photos to family members. The best thing about storing photos digitally is that they are easy to share with friends and family members; all it takes is sending a text or email, or posting on the internet.

If you look for a photo service to store your photos on the cloud, there are several things to consider:

1. Space – Make sure you get plenty of space for a low cost.

2. Quality – make sure that the service does not compress photos. Compression can compromise the quality of your photos if not done correctly. If a company compresses photos, look at a sample to ensure that the quality is clear and flawless.

3. Ease of Use – You want to be able to easily access your photos. Make sure you can store images in whatever order you like. You should be able to store photos by date, by event or by some other tag.

4. Security – While you want to be able to access your photos with ease, you also want to restrict access to individuals you have granted viewing permission. Password access is usually sufficient protection.

5. Easy of Sharing – You want to be able to easily share your photos with others and post them on social media.

6. Printability – You should have the ability to print photos either from your own printer or at a photo kiosk.

The following are some companies that store photos for you:

Shutterfly – Shutterfly has a free service for storing photos. It has very simple tools that make photos easy to print and share. They also offer paid services for printing your photos on calendars, mugs or other promotional items.

500 Pixels – serves primarily professional photographers. You can sort photos into albums, or stories for events. If you go to someone's wedding and take pictures there, you can store them in a story form that the wedding party can access and select photos for purchase. There is a free version of this softward, but the paid subscription includes all sorts of lovely bells and whistles.

Photobucket – is a free service that offers a whole 2GB of storage for a fee. This service has great editing tools that anyone can figure out.

Flickr – has a large selection of tools to work with. You get one TB of space free, as long as you can tolerate looking at ads. Viewing, editing, and downloading photos are all very easy.

Facebook – Facebook offers you the ability to edit photos and create albums. The biggest problem with this service is that you have to fit your photos into their parameters of 720 to 960 pixels. They do compress photos, but most of the time the images come out looking pretty good.

Google+ - Google plus uses some of the same features as Picasso Image Editing. It includes an extensive set of filters and you can easily crop and edit your photos.

CDs
MP3 players often store about 1,500 songs, which gives you the equivalent of around 150 CDs. You can play MP3s on other devices besides an MP3 player.

Most computers come with software that will rip music to your computer, but the programs are minimal. There are other programs out there that are either freeware or may cost a bit of money, but they have better tools and include the ability to store music in multiple formats:

- Fairstar's CD Ripper is a good and easy ripper.

- Exact Audio Copy is really good at filling in where a CD might be scratched.

- CDex Q is a free option for MP3s.

If you would rather have a service rip your CDs, you have several options. The process is fairly simple. You just ship off your CDs and they come back in any format you wish. Here are a few of the most well-known services:

- MusicShifter is a reputable service that will transfer several CDs free depending on how many you are having processed.

- dmp3 Digital transfers music from CDs to any of multiple formats.

- Riptopia performs standard ripping services.

Most of these services charge $1 per CD (make sure it isn't $1 per minute) and provide spindles on which to put your CDs and a box in which to send them. You get your CDs back in a few days along with digital files.

DVDs

DVDs are becoming a thing of the past. It is so easy to download movies from a cable provider or to subscribe to Netflix, Hulu and other services, that few DVDs are needed. You can now take all your old DVDs and transcribe them into your computer storage. Then you can watch them directly on your computer or you can hook your computer up to your TV to view on the television screen.

Some good video transcoders are:

- Handbrake
- Wondershare
- Zencoder from Brightcove
- Wowza
- MPEG Streamclip
- Super from eRightSoft

Some of these are free while others begin with free trials followed by required subscription. You can store your movies on the cloud, on your computer, and on other devices.

TV

Cable TV is nice, but it costs a lot of money. I recently ended my cable subscription and got a Roku along with subscriptions to Netflix, Hulu and CBS. Now I can watch almost everything I used to watch with cable and I can do it when I want to watch it, not when the stations say I have to.

You may have to wait a week or two for a favorite show to appear on NBC or ABC if you no longer have a provider, but other stations put some of their shows on Hulu the day after they air. I am now paying much less for just internet service so it absolutely saves you money, which is important for a minimalist.

Books, Newspapers and Magazines

E-readers are a great way to handle books, newspapers, and magazines. Instead of paper lying around in the way, you have the small e-reader to read them with.

Most e-readers will hold many different publications at one time, which helps greatly reduce clutter. In most cases, e-books and e-subscriptions are much cheaper than the paper versions, mainly because they include no mailing or printing fees. Kindle and Nook are the most popular e-readers, but there are others that also work moderately well. One of the best things about e-publications is that you can read documents on your computer and your smartphone, as well as on a dedicated e-reader.

Managing Your Electronics and Technology
Electronics can take over your life, so the minimalist needs to be careful that it doesn't. Schedule your computer time and only do one thing at a time so you do not spend more time on social media than you planned.

You don't need all forms of social media; focus on one or two social media sites. Reduce the number of times you check your email inbox to three or four times a day. Schedule your TV watching to include specific programs you value. Set time limits for how long you play video games. Because the main purpose of being a minimalist is to have more time to spend directly with the ones you love, submit your technology usage to any necessary restraints to guard your relationships.

Chapter 7: Five Items the Minimalist Should Always Have on Hand

There are five items every minimalist should always have on hand. These items have multiple uses, eliminating the need to stock a variety of household cleaning products, beauty formulas, gardening solutions and the like. You can do it all with just five things you probably already have in your kitchen, medicine cabinet and your laundry room.

While powerful, these five items, used individually or in combination, lack the carcinogenic and allergenic properties of most commercial solutions, making them much safer to use around children and your pets.

1. Vinegar

Vinegar is an amazing substance. It cleans, sanitizes, gets rid of pests in your garden, clarifies your hair, and much more. You should always keep on hand both regular white vinegar and apple cider vinegar. Just be careful to use white vinegar when cleaning fabrics, as apple cider vinegar can leave a stain.

White vinegar is clear and its flavor is very strong, which is why it isn't really used much for food. It is good for cleaning and for pickling however. Nothing works better to clean windows and mirrors than white vinegar. Here are a few of the many things you can do with vinegar:

Glass Cleaner

Glass cleaner doesn't just clean windows. It also makes microwaves, glass stovetops, and glass tables sparkle.

Mix 1/4 cup of 70% Isopropyl (rubbing) **alcohol** in a spray bottle with one half cup of **white vinegar** and two cups of **tap water**. The vinegar cleans windows and mirrors of dust, oils, and other grime while the alcohol causes the solution to dry quickly so it won't leave streaks.

Place the mixture in a spray bottle and spritz it on your windows. Do not use paper towels to wipe this off as it will leave little bits of towel and streaks behind. Instead, use black and white newspaper or coffee filters for a clean, smudge-free shine.

Floor Wash

Warning: Do **not** use this on wood or marble flooring.

Make a great floor wash by filling a bucket almost full with warm **water** and mixing in 1/4 cup of **white vinegar**. Mop the floor with this combination. For messy stains, like spilled jam or dried-on food, bring along a scrub brush to lift them off. Spills should come off easily after wetting them down.

Never use this floor wash on wood because it will strip the finish right off. Also, avoid using it on marble flooring because it will make the marble look dull and lifeless.

Cleaning The Microwave

I don't know about you, but my microwave gets really cruddy over time. Things spill and spit; the appliance is used so frequently that we seldom take the time to wipe it out.

An easy cleaner involves setting a mugful of **water** with a tablespoon of **vinegar** added into the microwave and cooking on high until it boils. Let it continue to boil until it really steams up the cooking compartment. Let things cool down a bit, then wipe out the microwave with a soft, moist rag. The steam should loosen all that crud so that it comes out easily.

Another cleaning method is to dampen a cellulose sponge with **water** and place it in the microwave. Spray the inner chamber all over with a mixture of equal parts **vinegar** and **water**. Run the microwave on high for two minutes and then let it cool. Before anything can dry by itself, take the sponge and wipe out any debris for a clean-as-a-whistle microwave.

Toilet Cleaner

First, flush the toilet. Then, sprinkle a quarter cup of **baking soda** around the sides of the bowl, above the water line. Follow that with a quarter cup of **vinegar**. Close the lid and let the mixture stew for about 15 minutes. The chemical reaction between the soda and the vinegar will create a foam, but this is normal.

After 15 minutes, use your toilet brush to clean above the water line and under the edges of the bowl. Then flush and you will have a sparkling clean – and sanitized – toilet bowl.

Drain Cleaner

Drains in the bathroom are a tricky thing. Hair and soap tend to coagulate in the drain and clog things up real good. This drain cleaner is designed to break up those clogs and clean out your bathroom drains. Practice preventative maintenance by using this drain cleaner at least four times a year:

- Pour one half cup of **baking soda** down the drain.

- Follow this immediately with one half cup of **vinegar**. This will cause a lovely little chemical reaction that will dissolve hair and break up clumps of other stuff in the drain.

- Leave this for 15 minutes while you go boil a teakettle full of water.

- Pour the **boiling water** down the drain.

Deodorize with Baking Soda And Vinegar

If you were to sniff **baking soda** (I would be careful about sniffing too hard) you would not smell much. You probably know about the tradition of putting a box of baking soda in the refrigerator to absorb odors. Baking soda soaks up bad smells and neutralizes them.

Vinegar has an acrid scent that is not all that unpleasant, but can be off-putting for some people. The thing about vinegar is that while it does have that initial salad dressing smell, as it sets, it absorbs other, more distasteful scents and leaves a "nothing" smell in its place.

Place some **baking soda** or **vinegar** in small dishes and set them in areas out of the way of children and pets. I keep a small bowl of vinegar in my bathroom and it keeps away the litter box smell, among other odors. It won't add scent to your home, but it will neutralize less attractive smells.

Candle Wax on Wood

I cannot tell you how many times I've had candle wax drip onto my wood dining table. It can take the finish right off the wood if you do not remove it correctly. Start by plugging in a hair blow dryer. Aim it at the wax on the table and let it go, sopping up the wax, as it melts, with paper towels.

Once you have absorbed as much wax as possible, soak a cotton cloth in a solution of equal parts white **vinegar** and **water**. Wring out the cloth and rub it back and forth on the leftover wax. It should remove the rest of the wax while leaving the finish on the table intact.

Whites, Smells, And Static

Use white vinegar in your laundry. Add one cup of white **vinegar** to a load of diapers and they will come out as white as snow and there will be no nasty scent to them. It also disinfects the diapers, making the baby less likely to develop a diaper rash.

Do your clothes literally stink after you've worked outside? If you put one cup of white **vinegar** in the wash along with your laundry detergent, the clothes will come out with no smell. Vinegar will not fade the colors, either.

One cup of **vinegar** in the final rinse of a laundry load will eliminate static cling from your laundry.

Clean Your Iron

If you use a steam iron frequently, you know that mineral deposits can build up on the iron, only to transfer in streaks onto your clothing. To prevent this, fill the reservoir with white **vinegar** and turn on the iron, setting it for steam ironing. Let it heat up and then steam iron a bath towel. This should remove any mineral deposits from the flat part of the iron and as well as cleaning the reservoir. When you are sure all the mineral deposits are gone, dump out the remainder of the reservoir and fill it with clear water. Steam iron the towel again to remove all traces of vinegar.

Eliminate Fruit Flies

I hate these pesky critters that come in with fruit from the market. They get in your house and reproduce generations of new flies. One way to get rid of them is with vinegar. Fill a glass jar half-full of apple cider **vinegar**. Punch holes in the metal lid and fasten it down. The fruit flies will go in after the vinegar and drown because it is too deep for them to fly out.

Bugs in the Pantry

Place a small bowl in your pantry or cupboard with one and a half cups of apple cider **vinegar** and two drops of **dishwashing liquid**. Leave it there for about a week. The bugs will go after the vinegar, fall in and drown.

Germinate Seeds

Some seeds have a thick outer shell that is hard for the little plant inside to break through. You can speed up the germination of seeds by filing down the hard shell in an area and then soaking the seed overnight in ½ cup of apple cider **vinegar** mixed with one pint of warm water. Plant your seeds the next morning and they should sprout in much less time.

Mealy Bug Removal

Mealy bugs create a foamy spit-like substance that sticks to the plants in your garden. You can get rid of mealy bugs by dipping a cotton swab in some white **vinegar** and rubbing it on the plant everywhere that the foam is found. Most likely the bug will be near the substance. Rub it on the leaf and stem near the foam and it will get rid of the mealy bug.

Stop Rust, Blackspot, and Powdery Mildew on Plants

Combine two tablespoons of apple cider **vinegar** with two quarts of **water** in a spray bottle. Spray on affected plants early in the morning or in the early evening and you will get rid of these diseases.

Detox Bath

Add eight ounces of apple cider **vinegar** to a warm bath and soak in it for about 15 minutes. Vinegar has an acidic pH and this will balance the pH in your body and leave you feeling refreshed and renewed.

Facial Toner

Make a refreshing facial toner by mixing one cup of white **vinegar** with two cups of **water**. If you have **mint** available, steep some fresh sprigs in the vinegar for a day and then add the water. Remove the mint sprigs before storing it in a glass jar with a lid. Store this in the refrigerator and use a cotton ball or pad to apply it to your face. Nothing is better after working in the garden or mowing the lawn and you are all sweaty. It tones your face and tightens your pores.

Hair Rinse

In a jar or pitcher, mix two tablespoons of apple cider **vinegar** in one cup of **water**. After washing your hair, slowly pour this mixture over your head, massaging it in with your fingers. If you catch the solution in a bowl instead of letting it go down the drain, you can rinse your hair several times. Your hair will smell like vinegar until it dries, but then it will not smell at all. This solution gets rid of any shampoo or conditioner residue that sticks to the hair shaft and it leaves your hair squeaky clean. It also gets rid of dandruff and makes your hair shine.

Ease Sunburn

Mix together four cups of **water** with a half cup of apple cider **vinegar**. Use a soft cloth to apply this solution to your sunburn and let it air dry. This will reduce the pain and minimize your peeling. If the sunburn is really bad, add one cup of apple cider vinegar to a bath and soak in it for 15 to 20 minutes.

Heal Bruises Faster

Soak a cotton ball in full strength apple cider **vinegar** and apply it to a bruise. Attach the cotton ball with a bandage or medical tape and leave it there for about an hour. This will speed the healing of your bruise.

Cold Sores

Apply full strength apple cider **vinegar** to a cold sore four times a day and it will heal much faster.

2. Baking Soda

Your second essential item, baking soda, is amazingly inexpensive and can be found in the baking aisle of any grocery store. Its scientific name is sodium bicarbonate. This substance exists as an odorless white powder that can be used as a rising agent in cooking. However, it also serves effectively as a cleaner, in healing remedies, and in beauty products.

Baking soda is very useful around the house as it removes odors from the air and from carpets. It has a rough consistency that assists in scouring sinks and tiles. It brightens laundry, provides a natural fungicide in the garden, makes a great toothpaste, exfoliates skin and gets rid of heartburn.

As a minimalist, you can replace a multitude of products with baking soda. Fortunately, baking soda is also available in bulk quantities. Here are some recipes for using baking soda around the house:

Soft Scouring Paste

For a soft touch that won't scratch, grate 1/4 cup of **Castile soap** into a bowl. Add 3/4 cup of **baking soda** and one tablespoon of tap **water**. When you pour in one tablespoon of **white vinegar**, it will foam up a bit. You can add a few drops of an **essential oil** to make it smell better, if you wish. Store any excess paste in a jar with a tight fitting lid. Whenever you need a non-scratching abrasive cleaner, just scoop a little onto a wet surface and scrub away. If you don't use it quickly enough, the paste will mold, in which case you can just throw it out. I never let it go that long, however, because I use it all the time; it's my standard cleaner for my fiberglass shower surround and the accompanying metal sink.

Baking soda, when mixed with **vinegar**, creates a chemical reaction that can help remove stubborn grease. First spray vinegar on the greasy surface, and then sprinkle on the baking soda. Keep your nose away from the resulting bubbly mess. Once the reaction has simmered down, get in there with a scrubbing sponge. The baking soda has a slightly abrasive quality that you can use to scrub away baked-on grease.

Carpet Freshener

No one likes a stinky carpet. If you have kids and pets, you know that carpets can harbor distasteful smells for a long time. You already know that **baking soda** will soak up smells in your refrigerator; you can apply the same principle safely to your rugs. Just sprinkle some on the carpet and let it set for 5 to 10 minutes before you vacuum it up. The results will be a fresher-smelling room. Don't go too wild with your sprinkling or you'll have a real mess on your hands. Just sprinkle enough that you know it is there.

Tile Cleaner

Bathroom tiles tend to become dull over time, so this should brighten them up. Wipe – or spray – the tile surface with some **white vinegar** and while it is still damp, pour a little **baking soda** on a damp rag and wipe those same tiles again. To remove the soda residue, wipe down or spray the tiles with water. You should be able to see yourself in the clean tiles.

Fiberglass Cleaner

Make your own version of scrubbing bubbles to remove grime. You can use this to clean fiberglass and any other surface. This solution is safe to use anywhere in your house.

Mix one cup of **baking soda** with one teaspoon of regular blue **Dawn dish detergent.** This will create a bubbly paste. Use a cellulose sponge to work the paste into the surface. You don't have to work in sections; just keep working it into the entire area.

Half fill a bucket with warm **water** and add one cup of white or cider **vinegar**. Using your sponge, dipped in this liquid, wipe down the paste. Little dirt-fighting bubbles will quickly form. Once you are finished with the vinegar solution, rinse everything down with water.

Opt For No Bleach

Bleach tends to break down the fibers of fabrics, so I avoid it. Instead of bleach, I use **baking soda** for both bright colors and for whites, to keep the colors crisp. Add one half cup of baking soda to your wash along with the laundry detergent.

Toothpaste

Sprinkle a little **baking soda** on a paper towel and dip a wet toothbrush in it. Brush your teeth as usual and you will find that it cleans and whitens your teeth effectively.

Dandruff Treatment

Put a towel around your shoulders to catch the residue, then take a handful of **baking soda** and rub it into your scalp. Rub it in well and leave it in for an hour or overnight if possible, then wash your hair. This might take a few repetitions, but it should get rid of your dandruff.

Split Ends

Take ½ teaspoon of **baking soda** and mix it with one portion of your favorite hair conditioner. Slather it on your hair, leave it set for a few minutes, and then rinse it out. This will make your hair resistant to split ends.

Exfoliator

Mix three parts of **baking soda** with one part **water** to make a paste. Apply it to your face in with your fingers and rub it in with gentle circular motions on your forehead, cheeks, nose, and chin. This will take away the dead skin cells. Rinse and blot your face dry before applying moisturizer.

Heartburn

Mix ½ teaspoon of **baking soda** in a cup of **water**. Stir it up, drink it down, and this should put out the fire of that heartburn.

Ease Bug Bites

Spider bites, ant stings and mosquito bites can be painful. To stop the hurting and itching, make a paste with **baking soda** and **water** and apply it to the bite. Let the paste dry completely before wiping it off.

Melt Ice

Not everyone knows that **baking soda** will melt ice. Sprinkle it liberally on sidewalks and there will be no more ice. It is much less corrosive to your landscape than salt.

Fungicide for Flowers

Black spot is hard to get rid of, but you can make a solution with baking soda that just might do the trick. Mix four teaspoons of **baking soda** and two tablespoons of **oil** into one gallon of **water**. Put the solution in a spray bottle and treat the affected plants in the morning or early evening. Spray every week to get rid of the fungus.

Powdery Mildew Cure

If your plants are suffering from powdery mildew, here is a solution that will eradicate it. Mix one tablespoon of **baking soda** with one gallon of **water**, one tablespoon of **vegetable oil** and one tablespoon of regular **dish soap** (use soap, not detergent). The vegetable oil will help the solution stick to the plant and the dish soap is toxic to mildew. Put it in a spray bottle and apply on an overcast day. Do not apply on a sunny day or it may burn the plant.

Cabbageworm Remedy

To get rid of troublesome cabbageworms in your garden, mix equal parts **flour** and **baking soda**. Dust your broccoli, cabbage or kale and the worms will not bother them.

3. Borax

The chemical name for borax is sodium borate. This substance is a white powder that dissolves in water. You can find it in the grocery store in the laundry aisle under the name "20 Mule Team Borax". It is useful for cleaning laundry and other household areas. It also has uses in the garden and in beauty preparations.

Antibacterial Cleaner

This will give you a cleaner with strong antibacterial power. Place three cups of hot **water** in a large spray bottle, then add two teaspoons of **borax** and four tablespoons of **white vinegar**. Vinegar by itself will kill most germs, but to make the antibacterial solution longer lasting, add three drops of **tea tree oil**.

This can be sprayed on counter tops, toilets, sinks, doorknobs, or wherever germ-laden hands will touch.

Wall And Baseboard Cleaner

Feel like getting down to the nitty gritty of cleaning house? Here is a wonderful cleaner that will make your wallpaper or paint look like new again. It is easy to make and works like a charm.

You will need a spray bottle and a couple white cloths to do this job. Cloth diapers or old white T-shirts work the best. Once you are finished, just throw the cloths into the laundry so you can use them over again. This will save money you would spend on paper towels, which you shouldn't be using for this purpose anyhow. Paper towels leave a gritty residue on your walls.

Clean out an empty gallon milk jug and fill it almost to the top with hot **water** from the tap. Pour in one half cup of **borax**.

Once the borax is well dissolved, pour the mixture from the jug into a spray bottle. The substance is most effective when warm, but it'll clean pretty well when cold, too.

Simply spritz the mixture on an area of a wall and wipe it off. You'll want to start at the top and work your way down toward the baseboard. Spritz and wipe until you've cleaned the entire wall. Borax has a nice clean smell and it will make the house feel much fresher.

Vinyl And Linoleum Cleaner

Put one gallon of warm **water** (minus about two cups) in a jug or bowl or and add one cup of **vinegar**, 1/4 cup of **borax** and two drops of clear **baby oil**. Don't slop this on the floor with your mop because it can be dangerously slippery. Instead, pour the solution into a spray bottle, then spritz and mop a section at a time. If the floor feels a little slippery after it dries, just mop it again with a little warm water on a fairly dry mop.

Carpets Freshener/Flea Deterrent

Carpets smell clean and fresh when you sprinkle **borax** on them and let them set. Leave it set for about 15 minutes to help get rid of fleas. Then vacuum the carpet, carefully emptying the bag outside to avoid infecting the house with any live fleas.

Mildew Stopper

Mix one teaspoon of **borax**, one teaspoon of **dish soap**, and four cups of **water** into a spray bottle. Spray this wherever there is mildew and let it set for 15 to 20 minutes before rinsing with clear water. In addition to killing mildew, this can prevent mildew from growing.

Clean the Toilet

Sprinkle a half cup of **borax** in a toilet and let it set for about one hour. Brush the toilet and flush for a sparkling toilet.

Unclog a Drain

Mix a half cup of **borax** with two cups of boiling **water**. Pour it down the drain and let it set for 15 to 30 minutes. Rinse it down with cool water.

Urine on Mattress

Spray clear **water** on the mattress in order to wet it lightly. Take a handful of **borax** and rub it into the mattress well with a damp cloth. Let the mattress air dry, then vacuum up any residual borax.

Get Rid of Weeds

Do not use this in a garden bed, but you can get rid of weeds between cracks in driveways or sidewalks by sprinkling **borax** on them.

Fruit Production in Trees

An old trick to make more fruit on fruit trees is to sprinkle one cup of **borax** on the ground around the trunk of a mature fruit tree every three years. A young fruit tree can handle a few tablespoons of borax. Borax releases boron into the soil, which enhances fruit growth.

Shampoo

Make your own shampoo by mixing 1-part **borax** with five parts **water**. Put it in a plastic bottle and use it as shampoo.

Poison Ivy

Pour about ½ cup of **borax** in a bath with lukewarm **water** or just spread a paste on your skin if you come in contact with poison ivy. Never use hot water because it will just spread the oils. It will remove the urushiol from most skin but you must apply it right after contact with the plant.

Roach, Water Bug and Ant Deterrent

Combine equal amounts of **borax** and **powdered sugar** and sprinkle it where bugs run. You can also use this for mice, placing the powder along the walls where they run. The critters lick it off their feet and are poisoned and mice just don't like getting it on their feet.

4. Hydrogen Peroxide

Hydrogen Peroxide is a clear liquid that is often used in first aid. It is also used to highlight hair, whiten nails, clean floors, and get rid of bacteria.

Grass Stains

Mix one tablespoon of **dishwashing liquid** with two tablespoons of **hydrogen peroxide** in a small glass bowl. Use a white cloth to dab and rub this solution into the grass stain. Let it set for about 15 minutes and then run cold water over the area. The stain should come out, allowing you to launder the items normally.

Clean Floors

Peroxide's bubbly action is perfect for cleaning floors. Pour ½ cup of **peroxide** in one gallon of hot **water** and mop the floor clean. You will not need to rinse it off unless the floor is really dirty.

Bacteria in the Shower

Put a spray top on a large **peroxide** bottle and spray the shower after bathing to prevent bacteria from collecting in the shower and on the walls.

Shine a Mirror

Peroxide makes a mirror really clear and shiny. Mix a 50/50 solution of **peroxide** and **water** and spray on a mirror. Wipe clean with a coffee filter to prevent streaks.

Cutting Board

Kill bacteria on wood and plastic cutting boards by spraying **peroxide** on the surface and scrubbing. Rinse with **water** and let the cutting boards air dry.

Disinfect Wounds

Use on small wounds. Avoid use on larger wounds because **peroxide** tends to harm cell structures. The normal frothing action will help loosen dirt, dead cells and debris so they can be removed.

Keep The Cold And Flu Away

Fill the bottle cap with **hydrogen peroxide** and pour it in your ear. The bubbling may tickle but let it do its thing for at least a minute before pouring it out and repeating the process with the other ear. Perform this treatment whenever you feel like your body is starting to come down with an illness. It will not hurt your ears and it may well prevent you from coming down with whatever bug is currently making the rounds.

Highlight Your Hair

Spray **peroxide** on your damp, clean hair and leave it on for about 15 minutes to bring out highlights before rinsing it out. This works very well if you go out into the sun on a summer day, but be careful; it might work too well and lighten your hair more than you want.

Teeth Whitening

Make a paste with **baking soda** and **peroxide** and brush your teeth with it. The paste will also freshen your breath.

Whiter Nails

Stop the yellowing of your fingernails by soaking them in a small bowl of **hydrogen peroxide**.

5. Salt

Salt is good for many things besides seasoning food. There are different salts designed for a variety of uses. Table salt, sea salt, and rock salt all have their different uses. Salt gets rid of odors, provides abrasiveness in a cleaner, prevents bugs from invading your garden, eases the pain of stings, and helps to de-ice windows.

Cleaning Greasy Pots And Pans

Grease on pots and pans can make for a real mess. Not only does it not come off easily, preferring to leave a nasty residue, but the grease can make them slippery, easy to drop and hard to get a grip on.

This remedy works well on metal and glass pans and casserole dishes. Note: DO NOT USE THIS METHOD ON NON-STICK POTS AND PANS, as it will scratch off the finish. Sprinkle the offending surface liberally with table **salt** while the pan or dish is still hot to warm. Let it set for one hour then dump any loose salt into the garbage and clean the pot. This method is good for aluminum, stainless steel, glass, and cast iron.

Oven Spills

Nothing is worse than food spilling over in the oven and creating enough smoke to set off your fire alarm every time you go to bake something. Should anything spill while you are baking, immediately throw some table **salt** over the spill on the oven bottom. This will stop the smoking and will let you keep on cooking. Later, after the oven has cooled, wipe out the salt with a damp sponge. The spill should clean up easily.

Stop Colors From Fading

Turn your dark-colored clothing inside-out before throwing it into the washer. This will minimize fading.

With new clothes, treat them before you wear them. Adding one cup of non-iodized table **salt** to the wash will slow the facing process.

Remove Dead Skin Cells

After a bath, dry off and while your skin is still a little damp, massage in some sea **salt**. This works great on the body, also on the face, but treat your face very gently.

Reduce Eye Puffiness

Get reduce those puffy eyes by combining one teaspoon of table **salt** into one pint of hot **water**. Apply with cotton pads.

Salty Facial

Mix equal parts table **salt** and **olive oil** and massage the mixture into your face. Let it set for five minutes before washing it off.

Ease Pain From Stings And Bites

Lightly wet the area of the sting with **water** and apply table **salt**. It will immediately stop the pain and arrest the swelling. Note: If you are allergic to bee stings, this will NOT help you. Wet a mosquito bite and apply table salt to stop the swelling and itching.

Poison Ivy

Soak in a sea **salt-water** bath in tepid water to ease the itching of poison ivy breakouts. Note: this will not remove the urushiol that caused the allergic reaction, but it will temporarily ease the discomfort of the itching. Be careful to pat dry your body afterwards, as the real healing comes from drying up the irritated skin.

Eradicate Snails and Slugs

Snails and slugs are slimy little creatures and salt does a real number on them. If they come into contact with salt, their bodies actually start to melt into a pile of goo. Sprinkle table **salt** under plants they like to eat.

Kill Poison Ivy Plants

Just as salt eases the pain of poison ivy, it also kills the plant. Dissolve three teaspoons of table **salt** in 1-gallon of **water**, add a tablespoon of **dish soap**, place the mixture in a spray bottle and apply to the plants, while wearing long sleeves and gloves.

Afterwards, peel off your shirt and gloves, avoiding all contact with the outer surfaces, and wash them immediately to remove any stray urushiol. I also recommend washing your arms and hands for two minutes using Dawn dish soap, just in case any stray urushiol made it past your defenses.

Stop Ants in Their Tracks

Sprinkle table **salt** across ant paths to keep them from getting into the house. You can also sprinkle salt across doorways and window ledges to keep them out.

Deodorize

Sprinkle table or sea **salt** into canvas shoes to keep them smelling sweet. Let them set overnight, then shake them out into the trash can in the morning. Note: do NOT use to treat leather shoes.

Deice Windows

Make sea **salt water** and wipe your windshield and windows with the solution. You can actually put sea salt in a small muslin bag with a drawstring and when it snows, you can rub the bag on your windshield. No ice or snow will collect unless it gets really cold.

You can see that these five items can serve multiple purposes in your life. As a minimalist, you can clear your house of the piles of bottles and jars that accumulate under the sink and stock the few key items that work every bit as efficiently. You will be detoxifying your environment and simplifying your life in one fell swoop.

Conclusion

I hope this book was able to help you clear your life of things you don't need and maximize the usefulness of what you keep. I hope the objects and relationships you hold onto bring you happiness beyond measure.

Your next step, now that you've finished reading, is to start the decluttering process. Declutter your closets, your pantry, your bedroom, and your whole house – but don't stop there. Declutter your relationships so you can focus on those that bring you joy and happiness. Utilize technology to further declutter your life, then focus on utilizing multipurpose items for storage, cleaning, first aid, and beauty products. Minimize the clutter under your sink. The fewer items you have, the less there is to worry about maintaining; minimizing can create the space necessary to experience the peace and satisfaction we all long for.

Now that you know what to do, get to it! Do what is right for you. If you prefer to do it all in a mass cleaning, then go for it! If you would rather take it a little at a time, make a plan and get started. There is no better time to begin than right now with something simple. With a little planning in the beginning, after you declutter your life, organization will be a breeze. Once you organize your external environment, it will be much easier to organize your inner life, giving you more room to experience peace and contentment. Have some fun during the process and go ahead and get started!

Finally, if you discovered at least one thing that has helped you or that you think would be beneficial to someone else, be sure to take a few seconds to easily post a quick positive review. As an author, your positive feedback is desperately needed. Your highly valuable five star reviews are like a river of golden joy flowing through a sunny forest of mighty trees and beautiful flowers! *To do your good deed in making the world a better place by helping others with your valuable insight, just leave a nice review.*

My Other Books and Audio Books
www.AcesEbooks.com

Health Books

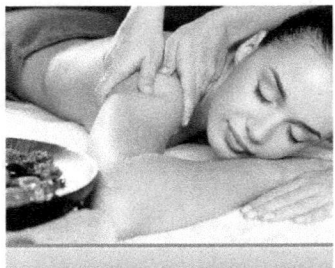

Peak Performance Books

Be sure to check out my audio books as well!

 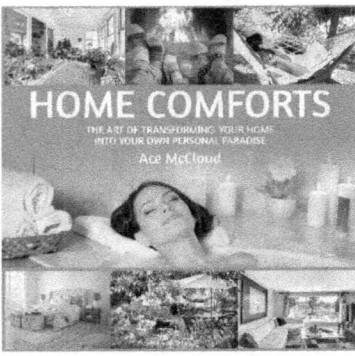 

Check out my website at: **www.AcesEbooks.com** for a complete list of all of my books and high quality audio books. I enjoy bringing you the best knowledge in the world and wish you the best in using this information to make your journey through life better and more enjoyable! **Best of luck to you!**

www.ingramcontent.com/pod-product-compliance
Lightning Source LLC
Chambersburg PA
CBHW051422070526
44584CB00023B/3538